Date: 1/18/12

636.7 PRI
Prisant, Carol,
Dog house : a love story /

Dog House

Dog House

A Love Story

CAROL PRISANT

GOTHAM BOOKS

GOTHAM BOOKS
Published by Penguin Group (USA) Inc.
375 Hudson Street, New York, New York 10014, U.S.A.
Penguin Group (Canada), 90 Eglinton Avenue East, Suite 700, Toronto,
Ontario M4P 2Y3, Canada (a division of Pearson Penguin Canada Inc.);
Penguin Books Ltd, 80 Strand, London WC2R 0RL, England; Penguin
Ireland, 25 St Stephen's Green, Dublin 2, Ireland (a division of Penguin
Books Ltd); Penguin Group (Australia), 250 Camberwell Road, Camberwell,
Victoria 3124, Australia (a division of Pearson Australia Group Pty Ltd);
Penguin Books India Pvt Ltd, 11 Community Centre, Panchsheel Park, New
Delhi—110 017, India; Penguin Group (NZ), 67 Apollo Drive, Rosedale,
North Shore 0632, New Zealand (a division of Pearson New Zealand Ltd);
Penguin Books (South Africa) (Pty) Ltd, 24 Sturdee Avenue, Rosebank,
Johannesburg 2196, South Africa

Penguin Books Ltd, Registered Offices: 80 Strand, London WC2R 0RL,
England

Published by Gotham Books, a member of Penguin Group (USA) Inc.

First printing, May 2010
10 9 8 7 6 5 4 3 2 1

Gotham Books and the skyscraper logo are trademarks of Penguin Group
(USA) Inc.

LIBRARY OF CONGRESS CATALOGING-IN-PUBLICATION DATA
has been applied for.

ISBN 978-1-592-40566-4

Printed in the United States of America
Set in Cochin • Designed by Patrice Sheridan

*Penguin is committed to publishing works of quality and integrity. In that spirit, we are
proud to offer this book to our readers; however, the story, the experiences, and the words are
the author's alone.*

For

Tucker Velocity Prisant

Contents

Chapter One: **Pseudo-Dogs** 11

Chapter Two: **Starter Dog** 23

Chapter Three: **Underdog** 33

Chapter Four: **Bitch** 63

Chapter Five: **Devil Dogs** 105

Chapter Six: **Dog Star** 131

Chapter Seven: **Dogged** 149

Chapter Eight: **Dog People** 171

Chapter Nine: **Dog Person** 211

Author's Note

Because I realize it can be frustrating to the reader to suspect he's mispronouncing the names of important characters—even in books that aren't Russian novels—you might like to know that "Millard" is pronounced as if it were "Miller" with a "d."

And "Cosi" is "cozy."

And was.

Our Juno___1994–2010

Pre-Dogs

True love is what we hope to be uncomplicatedly given by our parents and grandparents, by our children, our grandchildren, our husbands, our wives and our friends. We long to be beloved on this earth, and how lucky we are that most of us are born into a potential for unbounded love.

In my time, I have been every one of the above except a husband, and I think you should know—in case you don't already—that people are dauntingly prickly, and that true love . . . the Real Thing . . . isn't easy at all to find. I suppose I won't be delivering any news either if I mention that relationships are complex.

Husband-love, though, is especially tricky.

❄   ❄   ❄

The polls tell us that marriages are most commonly imperiled by money, by sex and, to a lesser degree, by in-laws. Simple stupidity is in there somewhere, of course, though most polls overlook it. And while my own long marital experience included at least a smattering of all these things — plus a decent-size chunk of some — it was true love nonetheless.

Which brings me to dogs and dog-love: the heart's great balm.

Dog-love is steadfast, unreserved and
   genuine.
It's wholehearted.
It's uncritical.
It's accommodating.

Come home tired and cranky, for example, and your dog doesn't care. Mix its kibble with chicken franks and kids' yogurt and holler "dinner" and your dog will whine in happy anticipation and lick the bowl when it's done. Make a tuna and pea casserole for your husband, on the other hand (and I only did it once), if you're newlyweds, he may, manfully, eat it.

My own husband, except for that tuna casserole, was singularly unspoiled about food. He didn't care to know the given name of the fried chicken he ate as long as it was accompanied by lettuce sandwiches on buttered white bread. He didn't expect a yellow and green vegetable every night, like a friend's husband (they're divorced now), and he didn't even mind that I didn't like to cook.

He did mind about money, though, unlike dogs, which never care how much you spend on them or on yourself.

Says Rover (and where *is* Rover these days, not to mention Fido and Rex?):

"You want to buy that fancy fleece-lined double doughnut heated dog bed? Go ahead. I'll be happy to sleep on it when the sofa isn't free."

Says the husband, "You want to buy a what?!!!"

Dogs don't care who you have sex with, either, as long as you aren't intruding into their space on the bed and as long as you don't kick them accidentally.

In-laws? In-laws just don't play a big part in the lives of dogs unless their owners are deeply involved in dog shows and pedigrees.

And dogs are simply *never* stupid. They wouldn't dream of telling you you're looking old today or getting "a little thick maybe." They always like your hair and clothes. They like their hair on your clothes.

Your dog—unlike your friends, who let you down; your children, who leave you; your grandparents, who leave you, too; your parents, who disappoint you—will love you faithfully, devotedly, unquestioningly, unto death.

If you get lucky, your husband will, too.

That's why this book is about true love and dogs and husbands. And dogs and life.

And dogs.

I know other people's dog books usually begin with some delightful tale of their first dog, the one they owned and loved through blissful, doggy childhoods and have enshrined in memory's pantheon. Maybe you had one of those dogs: always soft and fluffy, always clean; a dog that met you after school and carried your books home in her teeth and crawled across thin ice to grab you by the coat sleeve when you'd fallen through. I wish I'd had one of those dogs.

But this book has to begin with three half-dogs; the dogs that never quite made it, mostly because of my beautiful, inflexible, devious mother.

So it begins, then, with Sparky, a black-and-white long-haired mutt who scratched on our kitchen door one day, came in for a bowl of bread and milk, stayed for—was it three days or six?— and then was gone from my life forever. Sparky was a dream dog. He could sit and lie down and he could "shake," which meant that someone had civilized him long before we met. I loved his ever-alert ears and I loved his nonjudgmental affection for a five-year-old who dropped milk bottles a lot. Yet it seemed to have become quickly apparent to the key people in my house (myself not among them) that Sparky could also shed like crazy and howl like a lonely wolf, and that these traits were undesirable enough that his continued presence in our kitchen was becoming an *issue.* You won't be surprised to learn, then, that my heart crumbled in my chest when my mother told me he had run away.

How could he have left me and my bread and milk and devoted attention? And how could he have run away? He hadn't been out alone since he'd trotted into my kitchen.

I looked everywhere for him (without crossing

streets alone, of course) and brooded on his loss for weeks.

Of course he'd been a stray to begin with, my mother explained quasi-consolingly; why would I think he wouldn't stray again? But I had gathered from the reliable six-year-old source who lived next door that dogs were being poisoned in our neighborhood by a mysterious old man who hated dogs, and in my heart, I was certain—and am still certain in some childlike corner of my mind—that my mother, one rainy day when she wasn't playing golf—had put Sparky outside and the man came along and fed him poison wrapped in raw hamburger meat.

She liked dogs, she always said. And it was true that when we walked together down our street— she in her chic heels and a beautifully fitted suit and hat; me in my fitted scarlet coat and hat—and met a dog, she'd bend down to give it a gracious little pat. Though she wasn't comfortable about that pat, I could tell. She didn't seem to know a thing about good behind-the-ear scratches or bottom-wiggling tushie rubs. My dazzlingly pretty but frequently scary mother hadn't had dogs herself, and she wasn't at home with them. This was mainly, I'd concluded, because my mother liked a really clean house and a really clean little girl's room. ("Immaculate" was the operative word. I think she just liked to say it.) And dogs don't do immaculate. Nor do little girls.

Yet my next try was with a specimen that was as far from immaculate as dogdom gets. He was a big red Irish setter–golden retriever mix that I arranged to have "follow me home" from school one day. I don't think he had a collar, but I wasn't above taking a collar off and throwing it down the sewer. Anyway, this dog had a matted coat studded with burrs and big, mud-covered paws, and was only a little slobbery. Perfect for a sneak-a-dog, I decided. Though even stranger than my choice was my belief that the followed-home routine could slip past my mother's no-dog radar.

Hands on hips, frilly apron bristling, she stood in the kitchen beaming fury at us both.

"Look, Mommy, *I'm* not trying to bring this dog into the house. It was the dog's idea."

And possibly because the dog had such a big goofy smile, or possibly because I was so transparent, it actually worked for a few weeks—despite the fur and paws. She seemed charmed. And that was why I sat really still, nodding solemnly for the big, serious lecture about Responsibility and

Walking and Feeding, and then ran up to my bedroom to giggle deliriously and name my very own dog Rusty.

Ah well. Rusty turned out to be more than a little wild and not at all rusty, especially when you tried to walk him. Because he didn't exactly understand "walk." He was deeply engaged in "pull," "lunge" and "yank," and as happily as I'd envisioned the two of us trotting together down the street, the envy of all the neighborhood kids, he was simply too full of beans. Which was another problem.

Rusty didn't digest his dog food very effectively. In fact, if he was in the room at dinnertime, no one could summon much appetite for my mother's excellent cooking, and no one lingered over dessert. Nights that he slept on the floor next to my bed were spent with a pillow over my head and my face turned toward the fully opened window. Rusty's manners were equally off-putting and were, in the end, his downfall.

I think he might have even made it into a third week with us when, just before dinner one night, my mother caught eighty pounds of dog standing on the dining room table, long, golden tail sweeping majestically across the tops of the water glasses and just clearing the bread basket as Rusty polished off a quarter pound of butter and a bowl of Parmesan cheese.

"That's it! That's the end!!!" she shrieked. "He's out of this house tomorrow." And none of my tearful promises to be good, to keep him away from the table, to keep him in my room, to keep him—just to keep him—changed her mind. Rusty was gone when I came home from school the next day. I never knew where.

I only tried with my mother once more, and this time, the dog that "followed me home" was small, blond and appealingly cocker-esque. Also, it was a girl dog, which gave me reason to believe that *this* time, it could work. Everyone knows that girl dogs are smarter and more biddable than boy dogs. Easier to teach to carry your books and rescue you from frozen rivers. Easier to housebreak. Though the fact that I can't remember what I named her tells you how long she was allowed to stay.

Did you know that you can't get female dog urine out of wool carpets? Especially light-colored wool carpets? Until the day my parents sold their house (I was in college), that salad-plate-size, rust-colored stain remained on the bedroom carpet, about a foot from the right front leg of the chair my mother sat in to watch television. Who would have thought that little dog to have had so much urine in her?

Chapter One

Pseudo-Dogs

It was eighteen years before I got another dog. That was because, for the first ten years of my married life, we lived in apartments. Which is also why I attempted only two pets, both non-dogs. Not because the apartment buildings we lived in didn't allow dogs. They did. But because I thought a *real* pet—a dog, for example—needed to live in a real house where it could go outside and play or dig or find friends or something.

So I was twenty when I first undertook the sole care of a living creature. It was the late 1950s and I was a newlywed; a novice housewife complete with my very own ruffled apron and my Dansk stainless flatware and my deviled eggs. I had just fixed up our first apartment, on the third floor of what my dazzling new husband Millard and I referred to as our Victorian mansion.

In the intervening years, I had grown rather tall, and Millard was just enough taller that I could—wow—wear heels. He was really, really smart, too (of utmost importance), and surpassingly gentle, like my father. He had grown up in a town of five thousand in Georgia and that may have been why his first Northern report card referred to a "speech impediment." He said things like *sireen* instead of siren, and *mahls* instead of miles and y'all, of course. Not on his report card was the fact that he also had a lovable gap between his two front teeth and chewed with his eyes closed and ate ice. Noisily. But he pronounced Victorian just fine.

Though ours wasn't really a mansion, and it wasn't ours.

It was a substantial, gingerbready country house whose current owners, an older-than-we-were couple with three children, had cut into several apartments. Ours was the least grand, but its being the servant's quarters on the top floor made it the most romantic. Which is why, with the last of our five rooms painted in the colors du jour—I especially liked the part where one wall in every room was painted a different color (royal blue, sunshine yellow, and lavender in the john)—and with the plywood-door table lending us manifest magazine chic, I decided it was time to get a trial dog: a bird.

Found at Woolworth's five-and-ten and chosen from among twenty-five or so chirpy and much less attractive contenders, the parakeet I carefully carried home was shimmery blue with touches of mauve, and it pains me now to admit that I gave more than a thought to how well she would go with the living room walls. I named her Pretty Boy, after my grandmother's parakeet, although she was much too pretty to be a boy. Neither Millard nor I had ever had a bird before, but how hard could a bird be? Within a day or two of bringing her home, we knew we'd never have one again. Because one of her gray, wrinkly toes had fallen off. *Just fallen off!* I couldn't believe it.

Fortunately, along with my bird, I'd bought the twenty-five-cent *How to Train Your Bird* booklet, but found nothing in it about toes or feet or legs. There was a good deal about drafts, however. Had I set the cage near a drafty window? I didn't think so, but slammed each window twice, just in case.

Was the bird in pain? How could losing a toe not be painful? Panicked, I threw on my coat and sped back to Woolworth's for advice.

The flustered high school girl I collared at the pet counter quickly called over her nineteen-and-a-half-year-old manager, a smallish, acned boy, determined not to fluster. He looked me up and down. Was I trying to return a bird? Did I have a receipt? Was I a bird abuser?

No, no and no. I fell at his feet and wept. Metaphorically.

"Can you suggest anything? Do you have any pills? Any drops? We can't let her die!"

"You're probably not keeping the bird warm enough," he ventured, blinking rapidly and cracking a knuckle behind his back, with which it became instantly clear to me that he was out of his depth.

He set me thinking, though, for if warmth was what was needed, I could sleep with Pretty Boy if I had to. Driving home, however, I flashed on the image of one of us rolling over on a sick bird during the night, and changed my mind. So when I found her all fluffed up on the bottom of the cage (*that* couldn't be good), I gingerly carried the cage to the kitchen, our warmest room, and placed her as near to the stove as counter space allowed. Then I added some hopeful seed to a barely depleted cup plus a splash of fresh water. I felt a little better.

Pretty Boy didn't, though. By the following

morning, with her seed tray still full and water untouched, she allowed me to cup her trembling body in my hands while I placed her, ever so gently, on a washcloth I'd spread between the four burners of the stove, right over the pilot light. There she sat all day, unmoving, uncomplaining. But wasn't she breathing much too fast? Even for a bird?

Within days, despite my care, *all* her toes had fallen off.

It was painful merely to *see*, and Millard and I had a worried discussion at dinner about how to handle our failure in bird husbandry.

"Don't blame yourself for this," he suggested sympathetically. "Perhaps the bird was sick when you bought it. It will probably be better tomorrow."

But I didn't want cheap absolution. Even my grandmother could keep a bird alive, for god's sake, and by eleven that night, we'd decided to find a vet and pay for help—a real stretch for us. Though none of the Yellow Pages ads seemed to mention the treatment of birds. (Would you believe I didn't think to call one ad and ask?) The next day, at our local library, I looked for manuals on sick birds. But there was nothing. Or, at least, nothing that mentioned legs or toes.

In frustration, I sped back to Woolworth's,

where, after a second pointless conversation with the manager:

"Can you tell me what's wrong with my bird? She's dying."

"I don't know, lady" (defensively). "No other customer has ever complained of a problem like that. Why don't you try calling a vet?"

I concluded that five-and-tens shouldn't be selling pets to begin with. Shortly thereafter, they agreed.

And then, because Millard had escaped to Cape Canaveral on business, I was alone with that poor failing creature for three more days, beside myself with guilt. On the fourth morning, Pretty Boy was gone, and I buried her beneath a bush at the back of the yard.

After that, I stayed away from pet shops and five-and-tens for another two years. And the next time I went to a pet store, I was pregnant—and my new trial dog was a monkey.

A psychiatrist would probably tell you I was practicing: that the monkey wasn't a trial dog, it was a trial baby. The psychiatrist would be right.

Yet here was my rationale.

Because I was scared and inexperienced and had managed to kill or otherwise lose the only living things I'd ever had in my care, I thought a monkey might be a sturdier, safer, luckier choice.

In the movies, monkeys are models of self-sufficiency. Strew a few bananas around and they feed themselves; they're smart (a couple of hundred, left alone, might type *King Lear*) and well—like babies and dogs—they're mammals. And I'd never heard of a mammal getting fatal foot disease.

Besides (forgive me), I was bored.

You might wonder why I didn't buy a dog.

Well, I wasn't ready for a dog yet because we were still living in an apartment. This time, we were living just down the highway from Cape Canaveral at Cocoa Beach, where Millard, who worked for MIT, was on field duty. Sadly, he was spending what I jealously thought were far too many nights sleeping out at the Cape when there were "shoots." (Once or twice, to his great and lifelong delight, he actually slept right on top of the nuclear missiles whose guidance systems he was helping to design.) And often—too often to suit me—he would go out for a few days' cruise on a Polaris submarine. Therefore I was forced to spend much too much time by myself, contemplating the vast and boring Atlantic through the sliding glass doors of my second-floor cinder-block flat. Or sitting alone on our graceless concrete terrace, smoking (ah, yes, we smoked when pregnant then, and drank what we wanted, and on the whole, gave birth to babies that, despite our carelessness, somehow grew into six-foot-five, smart and handsome men with lots of wavy brown hair and absolutely no visible flaws). So there I sat, pregnant and smoking, gazing across the narrow beach, or "up-range," toward the Cape while I waited for a Thor or Atlas missile to blow up. They weren't meant to blow up, of course, but in my darkest heart I unfailingly hoped they would. It was always a much better show than a successful launch.

Anyhow, that's why I got a monkey. We were in Florida, in an undeveloped section encroached upon by tangled reminders of, if not deepest jungle, then kudzu, at least, and I was longing for a bit of close-to-human company. Monkeys, re Darwin, were closer to humans than birds, and possibly smarter, even, than dogs.

I got my primate at a local pet store in the kind of cinder-block strip mall where beach sand meets asphalt, and he came with no instructions. I supposed that when you live in a place where banana palms grow wild, it's taken for granted that you know how to care for monkeys. So there was no booklet this time. No leash. No cage. No one even to share the fun, since Millard was away again.

That meant I had to bring this adorably furry brown baby monkey home to an empty apartment, and immediately on entering the hallway, he ran into an open closet and crouched down under our clothes, holding his long tail between his legs and rocking back and forth and making this sound — a sound like a hurt child crying — that rent my heart. But then, as miserably unhappy as the pitiable thing seemed to be, he also didn't seem to be losing parts, and this was altogether a better beginning than I'd made with Pretty Boy.

I got down on my hands and knees inside the closet, and reached out to comfort the little creature. He seemed to think I was some kind of huge, insufficiently hairy hostile, because he skittered off into the farthest, most shadowy corner, where, given what was then considered my "delicate condition," I simply couldn't reach him. And there, I'm sorry to say, he rocked and keened all night.

You and that psychiatrist would conclude that if I'd been unconsciously looking for the pet that was most like a baby, I'd certainly found the ideal. I was up and down every hour that night, offering him cereal, cereal in milk, bananas (peeled), closet lights turned on, closet lights turned off, folding doors open all the way so he would know I was there, folding doors (almost) closed so I wouldn't have to listen to him cry, but so he could breathe. I lay on my bed throughout that night and into the dawn, afraid that I couldn't care for this animate, feeling being. Afraid that, like my mother, I might not actually know how to care.

When Millard walked in next morning and learned what I'd done, he threw both hands in the air (in what would become a frequent gesture during our years together), and then he got down on the closet floor with me. With a little teamwork, we managed to coax the sad little thing out with some segments of orange.

But oh, yay! Oranges! My monkey—it was, of course, my monkey because Millard wanted no part of this—unaware of any agreements we might have signed with the rental agent, snatched an orange section from each of us and holding one slice, humanlike, in each of his tiny hands, climbed up the (really unattractive) mushroom beige curtain on one side of the sliding doors and perched, in the safe middle of the rod, furiously gulping orange. After which, leaving sticky little handprints on the wall above, and holding on with his tiny prehensile feet, he walked across the metal balance beam of the curtain rod to rush headfirst down the other curtain, searching hungrily for more. But somehow, before we could feed him a few more segments, the monkey spied my husband's modestly hairy leg. Hurling both his arms and legs around Millard's calf and screeching, he held on tight with his sticky hands and peed, lengthily and joyously. After that long, terrible night alone in our closet, he had found his long-lost mother, and for an hour, nothing we tried to tempt him with could peel him away. No oranges; no fresh litchi nuts (my favorite snack); not even the bananas (what was it with the bananas, anyway?). Which was why Millard ate his breakfast that morning with the monkey strapped to his leg. He shaved and changed his shirt with the monkey strapped to his leg, and then I drove them both down to the pet store, where — when the monkey was ready and only then, and rather like the squid-thing that attached itself to John Hurt's face in *Alien* — he allowed himself to be detached.

That was my last pet for eight more years.

(Oh, all right, when our darling son Barden was four, we got a turtle. You bought turtles at the five-and-ten then, too — tiny green tanks with striped heads and red cheeks and decals on their backs of flowers or American flags. Until someone realized that decals were toxic; after which, they only came plain.)

You remember how turtles smell, though it's probably not exactly "turtle smell" you remember. More likely what you recall is the smell of those chopped-up dried flies in the cylindrical yellow box—the ones your child always forgot to sprinkle in the water so that, daily, you had to wonder how you were supposed to know if your reptile was starving. That's why you always took the precaution of feeding it yourself, thinking all the while about standing there in your newly cleaned kitchen, sprinkling dead, chopped flies (they floated) on turtle water. This particular turtle, forever nameless, was eventually released into the local park, where ostensibly it still lives. Grown to four feet or so in diameter and frightening to small children, it's sufficiently grown up, these days, to eat unchopped real flies.

Chapter Two

Starter Dog

When I was thirty, after ten years of living in apartments with no grass, no birds, no rustle of leaves (I swore I'd never live in one again), Millard and I found we could afford our first house. Rather, we couldn't actually afford it. A bachelor uncle had died, and Millard's mother, who had loathed me since I was seventeen and ensnared her only child, decided to use some of her inheritance to buy Millard—not me—a house. It was a homey Tudor in a prewar development—a little small, a little dark, with a one-car garage—but with a Japanese maple on the front lawn I could hardly believe was mine. Every leaf, every crooked bough, mine. I'd never owned a tree before, just as I'd never owned a kitchen or a fireplace, but after all those years in apartments, the treeness of that Japanese maple spoke to me of eight-year-old Barden playing in the backyard, of bikes in the garage, of Halloween, of neighborhood. And that's probably why, in overwhelming and buoyant suburban joy, I decided that it was time for our son to own a dog. The all-American dream, right? A boy, a house, a dog? Our family's moment to see Spot run?

Besides, now that Millard and Barden and I were starting our Real Life. (Yes, I believed that people who lived in apartments didn't live real lives. They were all just waiting in their various boxes—as I had waited—to be taken out and moved into their very own homes, with front and back lawns and a dog.) I needed that family dog to own and love till it got old, and thereby prove that my mother had been uncaring, selfish and an ill-treater of dogs. And children.

I'd made up my mind long before I was married to be a better mother than my mother was. To always know where my child was going after school; not to make his life a misery over minutiae like clean rooms and put-away toys; to be the kind of mother who cares that her son has the basic and necessary experience of owning and caring for a dog. On this cloud of maternal virtuousness,

I wafted into the local dog pound, because where I grew up, that's where one went to get a dog. (These days they're "animal shelters," an accurate euphemism that rolls a good deal more easily off the tongue than "pound," while also not punching out the mind's eye with harrowing images of impound-ed pups.) That's where I found our adorable little beagle—all floppy eared, small, short coated (no grooming!) and flatteringly licky. But before I committed my family to its first canine relationship, I took the time to look up "The Beagle" in the library. I was very much more mature now, and I wanted to know something substantial about our dog-to-be before I got him home.

Curled in a chair in my stuccoed living room with *The Survival Guide to Beagles* and *Beagle Training* and a mug full of tea, I came across the first of several characteristics that seemed mildly troubling:

"Slowness to learn."

Was that dog talk for "dumb," or did that just mean I'd have to learn to be patient? (I've read somewhere that patience *can* be learned. It's not, as I'd always supposed, an inborn trait.) Next, I found:

"Slowness to housebreak."

Now that, I thought, could create a problem for a well-intentioned dog owner—even a newly

patient one. (Don't forget, this was before everyone did crate-training. See p. 114) But, hey, I was
a capable, fully committed adult now: a wife, a
mother and a paragon of stick-to-itiveness where
mammals were concerned (yes, I'd forgotten the
monkey). I knew I'd be good—probably talented,
even—at housebreaking. It had only taken me
three years to train Barden. In fact, his toilet training had finally reached a point where the pediatri-
cian had delivered a nice little lecture to me that
ended with "But, Mrs. Prisant, I've never seen a
man walk down the aisle who wasn't trained."

And you know, I found that comforting.

But where dogs were concerned, my library
books cheerily offered—because the books I'd
picked were British—that all you had to do was
take a puppy out whenever it "looked like" it had
to go; or every three hours. Whichever came first.

And there was this, too:

"Beagles shed."

Okay, beagles shed. Didn't all dogs shed?

Furthermore, beagles were often known to be
"independent." Whatever that meant.

Millard was independent. Barden was independent. We *wanted* an independent dog, didn't
we? Not a Velcro dog that wouldn't let anyone go
to the bathroom alone.

This beagle puppy was adorable, though, and

remembering the way his pink tongue had practically permanently attached itself to the back of my hand, I couldn't begin to imagine that he'd ever show any sort of troubling independence.

And that's how, head full of imperfectly assimilated information, I went out and purchased the natty brown leather leash, the dog bowl, the Wee Wee pads (guaranteed to attract anything with a tail), a couple of cans of dog food, a squeaky Snoopy toy and a small bag of dog biscuits, and drove over to the pound where I'd pick up the dog my family so thoroughly deserved.

My plan was to surprise Barden with the puppy. When he came dragging in from school that day, a messy welter of half-off jacket, ringleted brown hair, books, shoelaces and gum and hit me with his favorite question, "What's for dinner, Mom?" (though it was the middle of the afternoon and, as usual, I hadn't really thought about dinner at all), I vamped:

"Spaghetti."

He grinned. Happy.

"But, Barden, come outside for a minute. I have something I want you to see."

And turning him around by the shoulders, I marched him back out the front door and down the four steps to our attached garage. He looked back at me with puzzlement and maybe a touch of defensiveness. Had he done something?

I reached down and hauled up the door to the carless garage and this little brown-and-white body came barreling out in a froth of fur and tongue and panting and paws. Catching the puppy up in his arms, Barden rolled happily onto the lawn as the day's dirt and Twinkie crumbs were licked, tongued and lapped off a beloved face transported by joy.

Is there anything like those first days with a new dog?

Everything about this small thrilling being, from those white, needly teeth pulling at your sleeve to the bristly softness of its fur, to the abandon with which it chases after a rubber ball, a piece of biscuit tossed on the floor, or a gnat, is enchanting. Ah, we were so in love — even Millard — after the usual, knee-jerk grumbles about "new," and "trouble" and "walking at night." Had there ever been a more sweet-natured, energetic dog? Not for Barden. Not for me, except perhaps for the moment when those little teeth sort of shredded the bottom of the skirt on the just-reupholstered club chair.

But Barden hadn't had to drag home some baffled but vaguely willing stray, then lie about

how it happened to be standing in my front hall
(though now that I thought about it, stray dogs
didn't really exist anymore, not the way they had
when I was small). I'd fulfilled his desires for the
best little dog in the world even before he knew
he had desires. I was unquestionably the World's
Best Mother. That night, he told me so himself.

Naturally, I set down — or thought I set down —
a few immutable laws. After school, without fail,
Barden would have to walk his Tippy (now you
know what his tail looked like) and feed his Tippy
without fail at night. He might also have to bathe
him. (Should dogs bathe?) This was just fair. If
a kid was old enough to have a dog, he was old
enough to care for it.

"Right?"

"Sure, Mom."

He was out the door and gone, socks bunched
around the ankles of his long skinny legs, and that
was the end of that.

But you know the rest. You've met Rusty.
You've met my mother.

Here's the strange part, though. Barden's a
grown man now, and he says he doesn't remember anything about Tippy. He doesn't remember
the surprise of that day, his joy; those fraught mo-

ments in the days to come when Tippy wouldn't come to him or me to be walked—even though I'm standing two feet away with the leash in my hand, urging—in my most patient voice—"Come, Tippy. Come on, good boy. We'll go walkies." (I learned that from those British books.) And he doesn't remember this little bicolor streak tearing around the house and up and down the stairs, pursued by his patient mother in trying-not-to-swear mode. And he says he doesn't remember me cornering Tippy at last, upstairs, in my newly carpeted bedroom, where he suddenly—intentionally?—made our walk unnecessary. Barden doesn't remember that he forgot all about the taking-him-out-and-feeding-him thing. For that matter, Barden can't recall a single one of those countless hot pursuits, or any of those walking, pooping, shredding, chewing phenomena.

What he *does* remember is the day he came home from school about a month after we got the dog (I hope it was a month, although I'm afraid it was more like two weeks) and was told in the gentlest fashion that Tippy had run away.

I didn't tell him what had actually happened until he was in his twenties, because Barden has developed into a man with a marshmallow heart and I didn't want to hurt him. Besides, he can really hold a grudge.

❖   ❖   ❖

Here's how it was.

Basically, I guess, I hadn't had lessons in Dog, and Tippy hadn't had lessons in Good Dog.

He, cute, happy puppy that he was, was just being a dog; while at the same time, stubborn, tinkly puppy that he was, he was destroying and despoiling my longed-for first house. What I didn't realize was that a solid ten sessions with a trainer would have changed both our lives, but I didn't know about trainers or dog schools then. I didn't grow up in a dog house.

And that's why, at last, in an act of desperation as impulsive as my original adoption of destructive, independent, shedding, unhousebreakable, busy-being-himself, darling, terrible Tippy, I'd called the ASPCA to come and pick him up.

What stays clearly in Barden's mind is that he and I drove around and around the neighborhood that first day with the car windows down while he called, in a voice growing fainter as the evening drew on: "Tippy! Tippy!" When I mention it now, he regards me with narrowed eyes and a reproachful smile, and I recognize, for the umpteenth time, that I did to him what my mother did to me.

I was just like her.

Minus the golf.

Chapter Three

Underdog

And yet . . . and yet.

I still found myself, somehow, stopping to pet every dog I saw. Perplexingly, it seemed necessary to my mental well-being. I found I couldn't keep away, either, from those page-turners at the library like *Raising Your Dog with the Monks of Skete.* Or *Dog Fancy* magazine. Or even the most saccharine of the Pup-A-Day calendars. Occasionally, too, as time passed and the painful memory of the Tippy fiasco faded, I'd find myself hanging around the entrance to the neighborhood vet's . . . like some compulsive, smiley dog stalker.

In the sequencing of the human genome, do you suppose they'll ever find whatever it is about dog addicts that sends them back for more? Could there be something in our DNA, perhaps, that cries out for those muddy paw prints on the new white pants or a barefoot walk through drool? Could this be why, no matter how many times you wipe up the dog-sick or are slurped on the lips by some fetid tongue ("DO YOU KNOW WHERE THAT TONGUE HAS BEEN?!!"), you keep returning to the AKC, the animal shelter, the rescue group, the backyard breeder, the grocery deliveryman's wife (see p. 172), for more? And could it possibly have been this as-yet-undiscovered gene (not from my *mother's* side of the family, you can be sure. That was *her,* yelling up there) that propelled me, two years later, back to the pound?

But wait. Before I cover myself in ersatz glory and collie hair, I have to backtrack a bit and explain, briefly, about my antiques business and those eight or so dogless years—before the hapless Tippy.

In 1965, back when Barden was only five and finally in school all day, my mother, the proud new owner of a moderately successful travel agency, came to visit us on Long Island, where Millard, having forsaken the world of unreliable missiles and nuclear submarine cruises to Holy Loch, had taken a promising job in the burgeoning electronics industry. We were still in our twenties then, and had been dazzled by the combined inducements of earning a little more money and living the Fabulous Life in New York.

Interspersed by not-nearly-enough horseshoe-shaped parking lots, the raw new development in a bleak part of Queens that we picked to live in was pretty much of a comedown. Every faceless redbrick building had its own asphalt playground, however, and there, on autumn afternoons, I'd sit on chilly benches exchanging canned mushroom soup recipes with women I seemed to have nothing in common with. Other days, when I could afford a babysitter, I'd dress in heels and a girdle and white gloves and take the train to The City to browse Best's, Bonwit's, and Peck & Peck and walk the Met until my toes blistered. Then I'd limp back to Penn Station for the dreary ride home. Though once, a car full of Iowans took pity on the overdressed young woman hobbling down Fifth Avenue and offered me a ride.

I took it.

I'm from out of town.

Across the street from our apartment building was a scruffy field where Millard would take

Barden to fly kites on weekends while I, grateful for a couple of childless hours, would greedily pore over the *Ladies Home Journal,* tuned in to the Saturday opera, or every now and then (and these were the guiltiest pleasures), cruise the local junk shops or get a temporary fix at the pet store. There, if I pretended I might buy one, they'd let me hold a puppy or two. This was before Tippy. Before our first house. Before Real Life began.

When my mother came to visit, she usually took us out to dinner at least once and had me drive her to Loehmann's in the Bronx at least once, where she'd treat me to a dress. This particular trip, however, after a day or so of rearranging my furniture and dodging all those fissionable issues between us—why she walked all over my father and why Millard didn't seem to like her and why she was so relentlessly competitive—she turned to me, and with the zeal of the newly converted, said, "You need something to do."

Still trying to run my life. Still gorgeously blond, hazel-eyed and beautifully dressed while I was still brown, brown and brown. Still intimidating.

But (damn it) . . . right?

Had five years of stay-at-home motherhood and onion-soup dips blurred my never-too-crisp self-image? I'd thought I really enjoyed the playground every day because I knew I was supposed to. I'd thought "Living near New York" was great, though okay, "near" wasn't "in." Was I poised yet? Adult yet? "Fulfilled" (see *Redbook*, 1965).

Um.

Naturally, I went on the defensive.

What I *wanted* to say to her was, "What do you mean 'something to do'? Some of us, you know, *like* being moms and wives! Some folks even find it 'rewarding.'" (Yay, *Ladies Home Journal*, although "moms"—along with "folks"—wasn't universal then. "Mothers" was the operative word and "folks" lived in places like Arkansas.) But I had always been afraid to argue with my mother-who-wasn't-my-mom, so all these conversations took place in my head.

I became very silent.

I was proud and happy to be a mother, I wanted to tell her. Hadn't I worked hard to be among the last of that pitied and despised generation that had gone to college to get married and achieve motherhood as simultaneously as respectably possible? Hadn't I washed diapers, spiked my child's orange juice with daily fluoride and pushed his stroller to the drugstore soda fountain for a pair of lonely ice creams? Wasn't that what Life was about?

Relaxed and beautifully groomed and sipping coffee in our L-shaped living room, my mother thought not. She may have been overly critical (she didn't like the way I smiled), hypocritical (she disliked all her girlfriends but told only me) and every so often off-the-wall mean; but she'd also become, unexpectedly, a walking, world-traveling proof of the merits of "something to do." Narrowing her eyes at the glass celery holders, Currier & Ives prints and owl paperweights that I'd been buying for three or twelve dollars or whatever I could save from my grocery money, and then at me, still wearing my New England pleated skirts, tortoiseshell glasses and frizzly hair, she had my eureka moment. "Maybe you should go into the antiques business."

In the sixties, married women who worked *had* to work. Put another way, they worked because their husbands couldn't support them. That was true for my mother and true, at that moment, for me. My adored father, who'd in fact *been* my mother, was dear, hard up, funny and (oh, I'm sorry, Daddy — in so many ways) under her thumb.

Millard was only the first two of these — though he got a smidgen funnier over the years.

I knew nothing whatsoever about antiques, but I was electrified by her suggestion. Empowered, you might say, because she would stake me, she said, to a serious amount of money — two hundred dollars. And I could buy anything I wanted.

I would learn about antiques! Read a book or two! (Like I would, down the road, with dogs.) Could I fail? Are giant turtles roaming Queens parks?

Then, having made things right in the pre-prefeminist world by dropping this bomb, my mother flew home to Pittsburgh and out of this book, and my little family and I drove back to Boston as fast as Millard could get a Friday off: Why Boston? Because I'd found my first "buys" there, and there were surely more. Still I did spend a little of my windfall in New York, or rather, in the five or so stores within a half hour's drive of our Queens apartment (one named *Aunt Tiques and Uncle Junques*). I shopped so carefully and with such focus, taste and discrimination, in fact, that it took me a full three months to spend my start-up two hundred dollars on sure-to-sell treasures like little gilt cups and saucers; a French bulldog pull toy;

a Turkish shoe-shine kit (all of fifteen dollars by itself!); a needlepoint footstool; a seated milk glass dog with one broken ear and glass eyes; and an assortment of flowered plates, several with chips. (Have you spotted that canine leitmotif?)

You'd think that Millard might have made some comment on, say, the shoe-shine kit. Something on the order of "Who in god's name do you think is going to want that?" But from our very first apartment on, he'd taken absolutely no interest in any of my curtains, paint chips, crafts projects or furnishings, vintage or new — except for his own, highly sacred, fifty-dollar mahogany desk. He was completely happy with anything I brought home. It wasn't that he had no taste. It was just that he didn't see Beauty. Which, if you think about it, is a good thing in a husband.

When I was at last tapped out, having added maybe another sixty-seven dollars' worth of inventory including, from my father, the much appreciated and sentimental gift of a box of my grandfather's unsold gold and semiprecious stone rings (my family were jewelers), Millard and I found a Sunday antiques show that for twelve dollars would allow me to peddle my "antiques" in a local parking lot.

That first day, we loaded an aluminum picnic table and a folding bridge chair in the trunk of our car, piled my treasures on top, each carefully wrapped in newspaper and stacked in the too-small boxes I'd begged from the supermarket (Millard was one of your all-star packers), and at around six A.M.—and on rainless summer weekends thereafter—he and I and little Barden (who began that day a major and worthless collection of discarded antiques show ticket stubs) left for some soon-to-be sun-baked parking lot, where the three of us would unload my "inventory." Then Millard and Barden would take off together for the day, while I would spend the hours from nine to five getting suntanned, learning that New Yorkers like to bargain and consequently, crying a lot.

"How much is that big Royal Worcester bowl?" says the stocky middle-aged woman with the balding husband in the cap and short-sleeved Dacron shirt.

"It's nine dollars."

"What the dealer's price?"

"Uh, eight dollars?"

"That's all? I usually get twenty percent."

"Yes, but I paid seven dollars for it." (Squeaky here.)

"But it's chipped. See! See on this edge?! Feel it. Maybe it's hard to see."

She holds the bowl up close to my face.

"Put your finger here. You can feel it, can't you?"

She grabs my hand, puts it on the foot of the bowl underneath. I think I may feel a little something.

"Well, okay. But really, it's not that expensive, and maybe you can have the chip ground down." (The sun is hot. I've finished the Coke.)

"What if I pay cash? How much for cash?"

"It still has to be eight dollars. I'm only making a dollar."

(Whining here?)

"Yeah, yeah. What do you think, Harry? Do you like it? You wouldn't have a pair, would you?"

"Gee, no."

"Well, I don't know. I really wanted a pair."

She starts to walk away.

"Wait," I call after her. "Look, I haven't sold anything all day. You can have it for seven dollars."

I somehow haven't noticed that the husband hasn't left.

"I don't have to pay sales tax, do I?"

"Not if you have a resale number."

"Well, but you gave me a dealer's discount, so why do I have to pay sales tax?"

"Are you a dealer?"

"Well, sort of."

"Then you have a resale number."

"But I don't have it on me."

"Then I have to charge you sales tax."

"Look, forget it. I don't need a chipped bowl anyway."

And it's over.

"Oh, all right. Take it. I'll pay the sales tax myself."

Which is how I lost money and cried a lot.

I liked the suntan, though (we did, back then), and I eventually learned to price everything a good deal higher than I really wanted to sell it for so I could reduce it. That's when I began to make some money, although it may just have been because I stopped buying cups and saucers and chipped plates and began to buy things that people really needed, like marrow scoops and snuff boxes.

By the time we'd moved from "our building" in Queens to that first house with the Japanese maple, Barden was eight and I had parlayed my start-up capital into a real business, a business that paid my dental bills and actually bought me the first of my old Humbers (i.e., English cars). In addition, conveniently near Barden's new school, I'd found myself a business partner; a nice old woman (she was forty-five) who thought she might be able to use a little help in her long-established antiques store in a pretty little town called Locust Valley — a town that reminded me of the silver-screen Brigadoon — utterly bucolic, complacently obso-lescent and so difficult to find that you wouldn't have been surprised to learn that it disappeared each time you drove away.

And that was how — and where — I became a shopkeeper. That was why my poor kid was forced to sit in the store every day from three fifteen until my four thirty closing — doing homework, eating the guilt junk I let him eat and reading the guilt comic books I let him buy. Not to mention those weekends he got dragged along for the shlepping and unpacking on the hot asphalt parking lots, and the frantic early buying at local school fairs where I made him sit on what I'd picked so it wouldn't get away. All of which explains why I began to feel he needed — *no, deserved* — another dog.

Have you ever been to the pound? Back in 1970, it looked like a prison camp and probably still does. Everything in the pound could be nicely hosed down because everything was cinder block except the fences, which were chain link and six feet tall. Each of the abandoned dogs lived in a concrete-floored pen with a metal bowl of water and a pan of permanently half-eaten moist food dotted with flies. As you walked down the aisle between the pens, all the dogs barked and yapped, but without real conviction: sort of like "Well, if you other guys think there's something to bark at, I guess I do, too." That is, all the dogs except the shy, sad-eyed ones who retreated to the backs of their cages and stared fearfully and never barked at all and the few mildly curious, silent pups that put their noses to the wire. Every time I stopped by the pound (I needed, sometimes, to pet a dog), I'd be reminded of those 1930s prison films where the inmates run their cups across their bars to noisily confirm their own existence, aware, surely, that it's an exercise in futility, though no guard would dare approach without a wood baton or gun. Here, moreover, you were permitted to, *wanted* to, reach a naked hand in to brush a cold nose or slide an ear or two between your fingers.

My pound's wardens allowed a kind of canine speed-dating. You could walk a candidate out on a leash to an enclosed exercise space where, ostensibly, you and your potential responsibility for the next ten or fifteen years could get to know each other. But you couldn't get to know each other, of course; either because the poor animal was mad with excitement at being let out of its pen or

because it was spooked and made instantly cata-
tonic by the unexpected nearness of its cellmates
and large, inept you, who was incredibly nervous
about whether you were holding its leash too tight
or not tight enough; about the fact that, jeez, this
dog looks a lot bigger out here than it did in there;
about whether you appeared to its watchful keep-
ers like someone who'd never had a pet and didn't
deserve one.

They knew about Pretty Boy. And Tippy.

Out of this hygienic meat market, though,
came Barden's beloved Fluffy, a needle-nosed
purebred collie: smallish, but, well—fluffy. He'd
been left at the pound by a family whose newest
child was allergic to dog hair. *They said.* Because
who, after all, would willingly give up a beautiful,
year-old, housebroken (!!!!) collie? Worse, who
would name such a noble creature *Fluffy*? Not a
name I'd have chosen. Not when he could have
been "King's Golden Knight," the grandish kennel
name that appeared on his papers from the grander
AKC. Yes, our Fluffy had a genuine pedigree,
which impressed ten-year-old Barden greatly,
as did the fact that this dog truly *looked* like—
well, you remember—the-dog-that-scrambled-
through-raging-rivers-and-forests-and-escaped-

the-clutches-of-dognappers-(with god knows what in mind!)-to-return-after-much-suffering-to-the-happy-domesticity-of-carrying-books-and-rescuing-children-who'd-fallen-down-a-well.

Nevertheless, remembering our noncompliant Tippy, I figured we might have a better shot at being listened to if we didn't confuse the dog with a name change. So Fluffy he came to us, and Fluffy he remained. Although as time passed and we knew him better, he grew a few extra names (as did all our dogs), and wound up as "King's Golden Knight Fluffy Crusher Dry Toast." ("Crusher" was Barden's; "Dry Toast" was mine. Predictably, Millard liked "Fluffy.")

The "Crusher" part was ironic, because Fluffy had the mildest of personalities. So mild, in fact, that it was next to nonexistent. Had there been a canine high school, Fluffy would have been eating lunch at the geek table. No cheerleader, no cool, lopsidedly grinning prom king, our Fluff. No grins or big, panting smiles from him at all, actually. Not like the ones you get from Labs or golden retrievers. No "Oh, boy, where have you been — I'm beside myself that you've come home at last — kiss me!" On the contrary, our elegant collie always seemed a little wan, a little dull. Lackluster, truth be told. Though not precisely Dry Toast. He didn't remind anyone of dry toast. That was merely a name I'd always wanted to try out. Sort of like Barden.

We took turns taking Fluffy for walks.

Millard liked to go around the block so the two of them could check out our neighbor's lawns and shrubs. Barden's preferred route (walking not being his "thing") was up to a mimosa tree about a hundred yards from the house. Mine was in any direction that didn't include Louie, one of the few other dogs in the neighborhood and the only one that lifted its leg on my shoes. He especially liked me in sandals.

Barden turned sixteen in our first house. He also turned into my closest, funniest friend. He was smart, and handsome in an exceptionally tall and formal way. During the seventies, for instance, when his classmates came to school in shredded hippy leathers and tattered jeans, Barden dressed each day in a three-piece suit and a pocket watch. (My father confided to me once that talking to ten-year-old Barden on the phone was like asking a banker for a loan.) He was entirely unaware of his odd courtliness; of how peculiar it must have seemed to his peers that he liked classical music and liked to spend time with his parents.

He wouldn't have cared, however. He was always purely his own person.

And when he was sixteen, he also went away to boarding school.

Millard was in the throes of starting his business manufacturing aircraft indicator cases (you don't want to know; it's a real conversation stopper) and had less time to be with me, so I was finding myself a little too dependent on Barden's company. There was our shared interest in music. My overinterest in his homework. My too-thorough knowledge of the littlest details of his life—his friends, his teachers, his stereo. And I was so busy making myself so obliging, so lovable, so thoroughly a pal, that he loved to be with me, too. Eventually, however, I could see myself edging into some twilight of the vicarious, and I decided to break the bond.

That's the sad thing with mothers. We painstakingly mold our kids into people we really want to spend time with, and then, just when the conversation begins to get interesting, it's time to let go.

But right before he went away and left me with no one to care about what was for dinner, I persuaded Millard—who had always seemed wonderfully happy to be wherever he was. Millard—who had never spent a moment contemplating anything resembling Change and throughout our lives never would—to put our house up for sale so we could move into something a little bigger, with a den and a two-car garage, maybe. Something a little more interesting and a little closer to my store: this last because my partner had decamped to Maine, and I would be alone in the shop all the time now—except for the occasional appearance of the rare customer who wasn't "just looking" and who was, therefore, interrupting my reading.

I needed a project.

Unfortunately, we found a buyer for our house immediately.

"Unfortunately" because it dawned on us right away that we must have asked too low a price. And Millard couldn't leave it alone.

"Do you think we should have asked more? Maybe we should have hired a Realtor? Would they have taken the house if it had been five hundred dollars more, do you think?"

Particularly "unfortunately" because we had no other house to move to.

The night after we accepted the offer, Millard was so distraught that he went to the liquor cupboard and grabbed a treasured bottle of brandy and drank steadily and straight until midnight. I'd never seen him do that—before or after—and I've wondered about it for years.

Recently, I've decided that it must have been because he dreaded Change more than anything else in life.

After all, he still owned the name-taped clothes he'd worn at camp, and wore them, too. Which tells you both how plump he was as a thirteen-year-old and how slim he became as a man. (Barden wears them now.) The college sweaters and jackets he put on every day to go to work had pipe tobacco burns down the front and holes in the elbows. Sometimes he had me take them to the tailor to have leather patches put on. If one or the other sweater or jacket wore out, he'd buy one exactly like it—same color, same size, same style.

I sometimes wonder if I had died first, what about his second wife?

But if Millard reveled in salvage and repair, it was because he was good at it. (And to tell the truth, my business only flourished because I could buy anything broken and he could make anything work.) He did our sewing, fixed our shorted wires, sweated our pipes, hooked up the stereo he'd built from scratch himself. His proudest possession was his giant cache of well-worn tools — all the needle-nose pliers; Phillips-head screwdrivers; shiny, scary dental tools; Black and Decker drills; Sears saws; wood-handled awls; and paint-smeared hammers that had been with him since boyhood. Each, he once confided to me, had its own personality.

We were putting together a stool.

"You know, I love this screwdriver," he said shyly, holding it up so it briefly reflected the fluorescent lights in his workshop: a medium-long screwdriver with a red-striped Bakelite handle. "It just feels so right in my hand, and the business end is worn down now, so it's perfect. I got it when I was a Scout." He smiled lovingly at the screwdriver, and I smiled at him.

But Millard got very drunk that house-sale night, so drunk that he and Fluffy and I had to walk it off in the darkened streets, passing and repassing each of the four types of Tudor and three Colonials that comprised our tidy neighborhood. We talked and talked about our future and whether we could afford our future and how things had been for his parents and my parents, and why it was that our own lives didn't seem to be as easy—as predetermined—as theirs had been. He was terrified; I could hear that in the dark. But he couldn't say so.

I was frightened that he was frightened.

Every now and then, when I consider the anguish my Love of the New caused my husband over four decades plus, I ask myself why he'd married a woman—well, a girl—who was the very personification of the "novelty-seeking gene." An original early adopter.

Unlike my apocryphal dog-loving gene, science has actually discovered that such a thing exists and that it isn't only real, it's also hereditary. I have it, of course, as did my mother and younger brother, and it's caused us all—and our patient spouses—endless trouble. But, frankly, after all these years, I've found it a real comfort to know I'm not actually to blame for my improvidence. It's chemistry. Ah yes.

Then, too, as much as Millard may have feared my dalliance with those sexy gods of the strange and new, I think he also liked it. For despite his own science and physics smarts, he was drawn like a moth to the right-brain life. In college, he'd actually made a point of taking music and Shakespeare and art history, subjects that didn't come naturally at all. And that, he'd explain in his fading southern accent to anyone at all who asked, was why he hadn't gone to MIT. (And why he'd only graduated magna, not summa cum laude; those Bs in things like nineteenth-century Romantic Poetry and American Art.) So while Millard never quite said so — as he didn't say so many things — I think he truly liked my antiques, my music, my movie addiction, my Patrick O' Brian novels: the impractical but scary waltz my wayward gene and I were always going to lead him.

I prefer to think that, anyway.

Within two weeks of that memorable night, we'd discovered and bought the kind of house I'd longed for forever: a nineteenth-century sort-of Greek Revival that — crucially — needed lots of work. Bordering a public park in an historic and partially restored fairy-tale village on Long Island, it had its very own freshwater pond (where we kept cannibalistic trout fished by poachers over the fence that divided us from the park), an icy, tiny spring-fed pool on an uneven brick patio, a listing wooden pergola, and several small rooms on four small floors. There was a spiral staircase to the basement, a front and back parlor, and only one bathroom, so we had to dash up or down when in need. Neither of us had ever been a "pointer," as in "do this, do that," and we both knew how to work, so Millard was the hands and I was the design and some of the brawn, while Barden, smart boy, was the kid away at school. And that's how, after eighteen years of marriage, we discovered a supreme joint passion and lucked, incredibly, into what would become our life's work: painting and ripping up tiles and painting, building period fences and painting, repairing rotten clapboard and floors, laying brick and painting and planting and painting, all in addition to gluing, wiring, cleaning and regilding wounded antiques. And painting.

Fluffy seemed happy in our new house. As the years had passed, he'd become kind of a perfect dog, with just a few small foibles.

First, he drank from the toilet bowl. Now not all dogs do this, possibly because not all dogs can. I'm sure those little guys would if they could, since what dog wouldn't prefer cold fresh water to some room-temperature stuff that's been sitting around all day with, probably, a few bloated dog food pellets floating in it. Not that I begrudge any dog a cool drink, least of all a thirsty one. But the first time I happened into the bathroom and caught Fluffy with his nose in the bowl, I moved so fast I almost caught his head as I slammed down the lid. "Out!" I shrieked. "Out, out, out!!!" (My mother returns. She'll be gone really soon.)

And when, still quivering, revolted and indignant, I recounted this behavior at dinner, Millard and Barden fell all over each other laughing; a really crude display of guy-ness that made me mad enough to request they not only remember to put the cover down, but put the seat down, too.

They did that for a day, maybe.

And forever after, Fluffy drank where he liked. Leaving the seat wet for me. Which they also thought was fall-down funny.

Along with that, Fluffy had intractable bouts of collie mania, a disorder manifested by a compulsive need to run in circles and bark when anyone left. (And that means anyone. Even distant, angry neighbors who've just come by to drop off a copy of *Barking: A Cure.*) Now this behavior might work with sheep, but it can be crazy-making for those of us who just want to go to the movies maybe, or to dinner, and who are truly tired of devising new ways to slip out the door without being seen.

Of course there's the old throw-a-biscuit-in-the-other-direction-and-run ploy. But Fluffy was never, as the dog gurus like to call it, food motivated. After one or two tries, it got so he wouldn't even turn around to watch the tasty biscuit slide — like a small beige slap-shot hockey puck . . . way . . . way . . . under the sofa.

We learned to escape through unguarded doors in the basement or to the patio. Whispering, occasionally hissing while attempting to squeeze through the smallest possible opening, we'd inch the screen door closed behind us so it wouldn't slam until we were safely outside, and then we'd break like lightning for the car, being careful not to scuff a single pebble on the drive. Millard had a couple of choice under-his-breath swearwords for if I caught a heel, say; I had a brilliant comeback for when he dropped his lighter. Then we'd open the car doors — slowly, slowly . . . and listen. Silence. We'd settle into our seats, buckling up, opening the windows, taking that first, deep, liberated breath, when — high above the hopeful catch of the engine — we'd hear that panicky barking.

"My sheep have escaped! Oh no, my sheep."

At which point, Fluffy's sheep would look at each other in guilty despair, turn up the radio, rev the engine, and like the poor little lambs we were, peel out to see something like *Born Free*, *A Boy and His Dog* or *Animal House*.

Or else, because we were usually dirty from the weekend's work, we'd just go to the diner and bring home a guilt-ridden doggie bag.

It got so that anytime Fluffy heard anyone's car keys jingle, he'd bark and run in circles.

Ah, Pavlov, tovarich . . . bravo!

Harder than that was the hair.

The collie breed has beautiful caramel and white, fluffy (yes) hair. Masses of hair. When the collie sheds—which he does pretty much all the time—the fallen hair starts out on the floor as a fine white drift and then, like spun sugar, begins to gather itself in bulk and size so that eventually, the largish clumps collect as milky soft tumbleweed—in the corners and under the chairs and on your sweaters and up the vacuum cleaner's hose. Parents of allergic kids give up on their dogs, but men who dress in ancient crewneck sweaters and khakis don't give a damn. Kids off at school couldn't care less. But my mother's daughter cared, and channeling her like crazy, I restricted poor Fluffy to the kitchen level of our four-story house. (In belated if ineffectual defense, you should know that on Fluffy's level there was a dining room, sun room, den and back porch). But what this meant to our sweet, obedient, hairy Fluffy was that he couldn't sleep near us anymore. And he minded that. Which bothers me these days. I liked Fluffy. I wish I'd loved Fluffy. Though never mind, Barden did.

And that brings me to the last of Fluffy's flaws: the sort of thing I couldn't possibly have discovered on our five-minute date at the pound.

He wouldn't go out in the rain.

Well, yes, he'd hated the rain when we used to walk him down our faux-Tudor streets, but how could he avoid it? We had the leash.

In this wonderful new house, however, we actually had a rough sort of "dog's yard" of grass and half-buried slates. But he wouldn't go out in the rain there unless someone — me, for instance — got all raincoated up and stood in the yard with him. Where he still wouldn't go.

Now we've all seen that movie I keep referring to, so we know that that legendary collie spent a lot of time wet. You can't herd sheep and not get wet. You can't bravely ford rivers without getting wet. You can't wind up all bedraggled when you're scratching on your tearful owner's door unless you've been really, really wet. What was *with* this?

I empathized with Fluffy, though. I really did.

Until one summer night, with Barden at home for vacation, with thunder and rain lashing the house and my nerves, I at last fell soggily apart.

"No more!" I yelled at our reluctant dog, physically pushing him down the stairs and out into the yard, where he stood—and stood and stood and stood—while I watched stonily. Guiltily. While he didn't "do" a thing.

Barden came in and began to beg.

"Let him in, Mom. He's never going to go if it's raining! Please. It's not going to work, you know that. Just let him in."

But I was tired. Adamant.

"No," I replied in high, conflicted dudgeon, my voice going tight in my throat. "He can't come in until he goes."

In fact, the rain was now pelting down so hard that going or not, I wouldn't have been able to see. But I wasn't merely tired, I was—as my mother said much too often, "sick and tired" of this. Sick and tired of contorting myself to suit, well . . . a dog. And as I was taking a deep breath, about to launch into it all, Barden did a remarkable thing. He opened the back door and walked out into the rain. "Then I'll stay out here with him till you let him back in."

If I'd been eight, I might have said, "Okay for you both," and flounced to my room. But I was thirty-eight. Did I want my only child—these days, my largish only child—sitting out there in the rain with a dog when he might be doing something useful, like playing Pong, all warm and dry and depressingly obsessed?

I didn't give in immediately though. I spent a childish moment spying on the two of them huddled on the steps in the rain, Barden with his arm around Fluffy's sodden fur, Fluffy looking off into the distance. Nobly.

They were wretchedness made manifest, two paragraphs out of Dickens. My self-righteousness curled into a ball and almost slunk away. But (I think) I'm proud to say that I lasted a full ten minutes before opening the door.

At around seven minutes plus, I was standing in the kitchen, watching the clock.

In life's revealing aftermath, Barden says that it seemed a really long time to him, too, but what made it hugely worthwhile was his glee in provoking an avalanche of solid maternal guilt.

I should never have made him sit in the store.

As Fluffy neared ten, Millard took a fishing trip to Canada with some business friends, and

Barden and I went to a Pittsburgh party. None of our regular dog sitters was free to stay with Fluffy, so I left him in a long-established kennel for that week.

When we picked him up on our return, he seemed thin and sad and more than usually lethargic. Worried, I called the kennel. "Oh, he was fine while he was with us," the owner assured me.

The vet we took him to called it kidney failure, or it may have been that we lost him to simple old age. But on the bridge of Fluffy's lovely nose there was a sore-looking bump that hadn't been there before: the kind of bump a long-nosed dog might get from trying to push through chain-link fence for days and ages and eons. I don't say it was the kennel, yet I know it was.

We shouldn't have gone away. I brood about that at three in the morning.

Chapter Four

Bitch

She was our first dog-love. The first dog that Millard and I loved beyond reason.

These days, I wonder how I could ever have been shocked, as I once was, to see a woman kissing her dog. But until Cosi, it would never have crossed my mind to kiss a dog. Kiss a dog?! Where has that nose been, of course. And can't you get fleas like that?

To tell the truth, though, I'd never seen anyone kissing any sort of animal. Not a horse, not a cat, not a hamster, not a fish. My mother had barely kissed my brother and me. And so I never realized that you could love a dog the way you love a child. How could I know? Until my own child left forever.

Until he made *me* leave *him*.

❀   ❀   ❀

Amazingly, Barden had been away from home for six years: two at boarding school and four more in New Haven. Those were hardworking years for us all. Lonely years, too, for the doting mother of an only child, though much less so for Millard, whose company was at last beginning to grow. Paradoxically, my own business was becoming less absorbing as I was increasingly finding pleasure in replanting our new-old garden and stripping paint and sawing pipes and getting all down and dirty. So much more fun than waking every morning to spend the day—and the next day and the next—in a shadowy antiques store with no Barden to make me laugh or go next door to buy us M&M's. So much more invigorating than the whole twenty minutes of fresh air I'd gratefully inhaled when I went to pick him up at school.

I'll admit it. Even when he was fifteen—a baritone with a five o'clock shadow—I picked him up at school. He'd become—I'll admit this, too—my male Galatea. During all those drives to and from middle school and early high school, all those hours together in the store, I'd been—consciously and unconsciously—molding his values, tweaking his good mind, honing his already wicked sense of humor to my own idiosyncratic specs, so that, when I'd finished this masterwork at last, who'd have blamed me for wanting to enjoy my creation for a little while? For more than a little while? For far too long?

Yet who knew the store would seem so pointless without him?

That was why I felt incredibly lucky to have this project, this personal *This Old House*. Without it, I'd have been suffering serious empty-store syndrome. I was particularly grateful to be able to hand my business on, too—in all its boredom and possibility—to an unwitting but deserving former customer.

Though I still shopped. Because shopping for antiques seems to be something I can't outgrow or unlearn any more than I can unlearn how to read. Even now, I'll come to a screeching stop for a peripherally glimpsed "-tiques" sign. (Though mostly they're "bou-tiques" or worse, "antique boutiques.") Or, I'll be watching a horror film and everything in some crazed, demonic house will be blowing up, and as it's all flying across the screen, I'll be sitting there, thinking, "Nice table!"

You can't keep an old dog—in the spirit of this book—down.

Nevertheless, I did take my fifteen or so years of experience, plus the remnants of my loneliness, and channel them into appraisal work, a specialty that was as tedious to me as taking inventory in an appliance store or practicing cost accounting, but which nicely supported my dental habit and frequent trips to Loehmann's. To anyone who asked, I explained that appraising was considerably easier on the back than hoisting highboys, which it was. But I never mentioned the 148 forty-pound boxwoods that Millard and I planted in three excruciating days. Or the four cans of paint I could carry from the driveway to the attic. Easily.

We were contentedly dogless during those years. After a decade with Fluffy, we were enjoying our freedom.

Should I be ashamed to say that?

Well, we had no hairs in the canned-fruit three-color Jell-O mold anymore. No forced marches in the rain. No dribbled surprises on my toilet seat. Just jump in the car and out to play. Should I be ashamed? Hmm.

Have you noticed that even for dog addicts, life provides naturally occurring dogless periods? Many people use that downtime to travel. Many can't bear replacing the friend they've lost and soldier sadly on. Some, like us, become too busy and fulfilled to need or want much else. Except, okay, for Barden to come home.

When he returned from college at last, accomplished, complete, awash in new friends and words like "hermeneutic," we worried. He had zip interest in law or medical school and basically, nothing to do. No "career path." No what they used to call a "calling." Astonishingly, none of the three of us supposedly bright and resourceful people had given very much thought to what kind of living could be made with a degree in art history.

It was 1982. One of our friends had recently purchased a "home computer" (she stored her recipes on it), but no one—meaning Millard—believed that the computer had much of a domestic future. This was possibly because, back in the fifties, he had taken a course at MIT in the Turing machine, the computer's precursor. He'd been so bored by those relentless zeros and ones that for the first time in his academic life, he'd actually dropped a course. Barden, on the other hand, had a pretty good idea of what computers could do and what they were for, and one late spring night in a cracked and comfy pseudo-leather booth at our local pizza place, he explained it all to us.

"So you mean," said Millard, "that I could store something like my inventory and sales in a computer?"

"So you mean," I said, "that you could put all the prices for anything you've sold or appraised into a computer and compare them?"

"So I mean," Barden said, "that though you'd always need someone to put the information in the computer, to 'enter the data,' you could certainly put your inventory and sales in a computer, Dad. Though the whole field of antiques, Mom"—he turned to me—"would be just too huge to get sales information about. Maybe too varied, too. But," he continued, "with something like publicly sold paintings, say, you could type in the size, subject, artist's name and whether a picture was an oil or a watercolor, was painted on canvas or on paper, plus the price it sold for, and if anyone asked you about a similar work— in a keystroke or two—you could provide them with comparable sales."

Well, he didn't lay it out quite that precisely, but omigod!

Suddenly, the seedy restaurant was bathed in Archimedean light! He had just described . . . a business!!

(Have I mentioned the novelty-seeking gene?)

❀   ❀   ❀

That's how Barden, at twenty-two, and I, at forty-four, became president and vice president of an art data retrieval company accessed by an 800 number and paid for on a credit card. We were the first art database. He knew nothing about the business and intricacies of the art world, and I knew next to nothing; nevertheless, we incorporated ourselves, advertised in *The New York Times*, and while managing to fumpfer our way through a surprisingly successful start . . . national publicity (the mother-and-son thing) and many more excellent and intelligent customers than we deserved . . . we also managed to anger the art establishment. Or at least those who weren't falling down laughing.

Our corporate "headquarters" was a small office in an old house in the historic business district of our little village, about half a block from our house. After those first exciting months, when we'd get to the office at daybreak, I'd walk over to be at the phones by nine, while Barden, some kind of delayed adolescence kicking in, would take his time getting up, shaving, having breakfast, calling his friends and ambling on down to work at, say, nine thirty or ten. Once he'd arrived, well . . . I was bad:

"Did you call back that guy from Chubb? Why not?"

"Did you write that letter we talked about?"

"What's happening with Mr. Smike in LA?"

"Have we heard anything from Bendix?"

Ordinary inquiries that seemed to me to be innocent information gathering.

Millard and I, after all, had been fairly successfully communicating this way for twenty-five years (well, not all the time). But between mother and wholly grown son. . . . I know, I know.

Even though we were both pretty much fried by having to deal with months of phone calls and research and invoices, I was being a nag, not a business partner. I bit my tongue until my mouth filled with metaphoric blood, but even now I can't think of a better way to ask a business-related question. Leave notes, I guess.

And that's what it came to, at last.

Millard and I had invested a meaningful sum in this start-up—more than $200, anyway—and as the partnership worsened, we'd lay awake late at night.

Barden was *very* young. He'd had absolutely no experience in the business world and his parents not much more, but we at least had age. Which is supposed to bring maturity and confidence.

And sometimes does.

The president of this so-far-successful corporation, on the other hand, hated to express an opinion to a client. Sheer hubris, he said, for some fresh-out-of-college kid to presume to advise anyone about art. He believed we should stick to straight comparables, not venture opinions. Whereas I, full of possibly dubious, semi-useful information, couldn't wait to pass it on.

Oh, he was right. He was embarrassed about his youth and ought to have been. And except for business-crippling snags like those cold calls he couldn't bring himself to make, I might have left him alone. But the noodge in me just didn't understand why he couldn't phone the big insurance companies or the corporate curators to make a pitch. *Business Week* and *The Wall Street Journal,* after all, were raving about his concept. And let's not forget the Japanese, who flew him to Tokyo to see if he could hold enough saki to be a trustworthy associate. The Japanese had no idea that back at his firm's huge corporate headquarters, if some dentist in Iowa didn't like said-president's scrupulously selected comparables and decided not to pay, said-president would not only take it really, really personally, but find it too painful to call to complain. Or that, for a full fifteen years afterward, the CEO would refuse to apply for membership in an appraisal group that had called us on the carpet early on. (I've mentioned he could hold a grudge.) He was honorable and sweet and naïve and young. Oh, young. And he'd had a fabulous idea that was being executed—in every sense of the word—by a pair of tyros: one of them an overcontrolling mother who, more often than was strictly necessary, wanted to know if her business partner had done his homework.

Still, give us credit. We lasted two full years.

During which Barden became more and more sullen. Conferred with me less and less. Needled me more and more until both of us revisited unlovely adolescence and I became the younger of the two. So, in the end, he forced me into a breakup. I gave him back his fraternity pin; he gave me back my loneliness.

Although maybe it wasn't intentional. I'll never know, because we never mention it.

"This is so awful," I wept as I prepared to leave our office for the last time. "How will you do this alone?"

"It'll be fine," Barden replied, eyes focused on

the third-tier Belgian landscape on the wall above my shoulder. "I need to make my own mistakes."

And I suppose he did.

In the decades since, I never again brought up the subject of his business. Never asked how it was doing. Never was asked for advice. Never butted in.

Talk about the taste of metaphoric blood.

Then one day, Barden told us he was moving to Manhattan.

I died.

And that's how we got Cosi.

She was a shiny white Jack Russell terrier with medium-size brown spots, and Cosi Fan Tutte was her name. (My choice, of course. You know I'm good with names.)

Why a Jack Russell?

I'd once thrilled to a lovably stubby JR, chasing a ball on the lawn of a client's house. I'd never seen another dog like it: so small, so pettable and well-behaved and *so* appealingly short-haired. I didn't realize how sort-of-rare they were in this country back then (this was 1984). I didn't realize, either, that a person couldn't just decide she wanted this or that breed of dog and then run down to the dog shop and get one.

No. One had to buy her by mail from a breeder because—and here's the thing about deciding you want a Jack Russell puppy or a Chow puppy or a Chinese hairless—whether you live on Long Island or in St. Louis, the nearest litter will be in Oklahoma or Minneapolis or in this case, Plano, Texas. Which means you'll never get an eyes-on look at the parents the way my *Raising Your Dog* books suggest. Well, photos can be sent, of course, but how do *I* look in the photos I send to strangers?

Though why, you might ask, am I sending photos to strangers?

(Later.)

Still, it won't be like buying a puppy from a cardboard box at a school fair.

There'll be none of those love-at-first-sight moments with a mail-order dog, unless you believe that glimpsing your life's new partner through the air holes of a plastic carrier at an airport freight depot is conducive to love at first sight. In my case, though, it sort of was. I was *so* ready for this dog.

Millard, on the other hand, who missed Barden but who'd never been much for hovering *or* dogs, had initially countered with his knee-jerk argument thing: "What do you want another dog for?

Think of our freedom. Think of the hair. Think of the rain."

I'd thought. For half a minute.

Cosi was one of those bandy-legged, tending-to-plump Jack Russells: a pudge. Today they breed them with longer legs, longer noses and, one is regularly reassured by breeders, owners, and aficionados, better temperaments. They call them Parson Russells, too, which is a disgustingly politically correct thing to do to a helpless Jack. Though, yes, the originator of the type—it wasn't considered a breed then—was a Parson John Russell. Still, your plain old "Jack" seemed then, and seems now, fine with retro sorts like me.

My Millard, who hadn't wanted another dog, hadn't thought I should buy one sight unseen and absolutely not through the mail, who'd seldom even stopped to pet a strange dog unless it nosed him . . . hard . . . adored her from the moment she bloodied his hand with her pointy milk teeth.

But that figured.

The shiny pages of magazines like *Country Life* are filled with grizzled oldsters tramping along English lanes trailed by tough little, scarred little, off-leash Jacks. Because Jack Russells are a Real

Man's dog. Feisty, willful, only incidentally cuddly and plenty mean.

Yet Cosi became our joint hearts' dog. We welcomed her beneath the covers of our bed (which was when I gave up nightgowns for pajamas), and bribed her with treats to hop on one or another of our laps—nose on our knees, head on her paws—while we read the paper, talked on the phone, watched the news, sat on the back porch, ate. Our sex life became a little dodgy since we had to put her forcibly out of the bedroom and learn to ignore the insistent scratch of her nails on the historic woodwork while having also to listen to the simultaneous high-pitched barks, pitiable whines, extended howls and doggy Greek chorus with which she announced to the neighborhood that Carol and Millard were doing it again.

Still, when Cosi sprawled in her accustomed puppy-lay posture on the floor (both back legs extended flat out behind), she almost made it up to me that she was merely our substitute child: that our son was gone from my life. Especially in the dusk of a mild summer evening, when Millard and I would take her for a ride to the local Dairy Queen to buy her her own (small) cup of vanilla. ("Sprinkles?" the owner would ask. "No sprinkles. It's for the dog. She's driving.") After which, head lolling on my knees, belly taut with soft serve, wide brown eyes blinking in glazed stupefaction, she'd sigh and wriggle down in my lap to be even more comfortable for the short drive home.

Cosi adored the car. Her single serious reservation about the car was that it seemed to attract her nemesis, the deadly gas station attendant. The merest glimpse of her enemy, relentlessly intent on forcing his uniformed way into her pack's traveling den, would make her strip her teeth and hurl her body at the window, frantic to kill. Far more often than either of us cared for, the service station guys would find her hugely funny, and as they'd stand and wait for the tank to fill, they'd snigger at Cosi's futile malevolence or, worse yet, tap on the glass. Ultimately, the rear windows of our car just above the gas cap were permanently etched with furious flights of nose juice.

Our quirky antique house was right on the village street—Main Street, believe it or not—and by the time of Cosi's arrival, it had acquired a Millard-built white picket fence and a Millardrepaired gray wooden stoop. Our mail arrived through a Millard-installed brass slot in the door, and as it slithered through, it made tiny rustly sounds that caused Cosi, sleeping a mere three floors away, to start, race to the hall and gleefully tear to death whatever she couldn't eat. Daily, the residue of glossy catalogues, costly magazines and soon-to-be-overdue bills bestrewed our narrow hall floor, giving graphic meaning to the dog-ate-my-homework trope.

We discovered, too, that she loathed other dogs almost as much as she loathed Gulf uniforms and *House Beautiful.* Sometimes, deliberately courting trouble, Millard would lounge on our wooden stoop with Cosi sprawled watchfully across his lap. As an enemy dog and its owner strolled unconcernedly by, faster than a speeding bullet, she'd be out the gate and down the street, murder in her happy heart. And my mild Millard — chuckling indulgently — would just amble on over and peel her off the unsuspecting and forever-traumatized Scottie or Akita and apologize to its terrified walker before hurrying back to brag to me about the latest derring-do. Cosi's bitchiness went straight to something I never suspected in Millard's gentle heart.

I wish I could tell you he loved my own as much.

❧   ❧   ❧

Millard loved our old house, though, almost
as much as he loved that dog. It was a house that
was genuinely At One with Nature. It welcomed
mouse births in the bathtub, literal bats in the attic, and every spring, all over the garden—among
the tulips, on the lawn, in the shrubs—wild ducks
holding orgies.

Mallards mated everywhere we looked.

There was one three way, in particular, that
were regulars; a group comprising two fat irides-
cent males and a scrawny, exhausted brown female.
Why those pompous, sleek drakes thought she was
hot, I never knew, but they pursued her relentlessly
around our house and yard, and if one wasn't rav-
ishing her, the two of them were noisily fighting for
her favors as she stood mildly, unconcernedly by,
preening what was left of her tail. We called them
May, Nage, and Trois, and they were our daily
laugh, except that the beauteous May-May seemed
to be kept so busy satisfying her admirers that she
seldom found time to eat and was pitiably thin. So
when we could get her off by herself, which wasn't
often, we fed her seven-grain bread and birdseed.
To help her conserve her strength.

❧   ❧   ❧

It was a real coincidence that we'd attracted mallards particularly. There *were* other types of ducks around the village pond and in the park, mainly Muscovys and domestic white ducks, plus, which won't surprise you, a hodgepodge of "blends" of the three. Multicultural ducks wandered in and out of our gate freely, but only the mallards stayed to play. This was coincidental because at fourteen, when Millard had been sent North to boarding school, the boys there had named him "Duck"; short for "Mallard Duck, the Georgia Quacker."

All right, it's funny.

But it always hurt me for the boy he was. I knew it hadn't been meant kindly.

"Duck" had mallards now.

One spring weekend, I came back from a plant nursery with water lilies for the pond. About two feet below its near edge, there was a neat, narrow shelf, and Millard and I lovingly lowered onto it three heavy pots with their hopeful shoots, tamping down the soil, fluffing up the stems. Every evening for a week or so when he came home from work, we'd walk down to see a new leaf unfurled and floating on the water. And one day, we finally saw a bud, then another, till there were five, promising and green and long, like buoyant spindles. We could smell those star-white blooms.

I was cutting scallions in the kitchen and happened to glance out the window at the pond when I saw—on the ledge by the lawn, May-May, Nage and Trois doing their thing in our prized aquatic plants. In fact, standing in the water, right *in* the lily pots, was Nage, holding May-May down by her now nearly featherless neck while Trois had his way with her. At the borders of their duckish frenzy, shreds of crisp pale leaves seemed to be . . . loose and floating toward the center of the pond, and oh no . . . was that a bud? I slammed out the screen door and charged down two flights of stairs, shooing furiously. Though I wasn't in time. Our lilies were destroyed.

Gasping and breathless, I raced back to the house, grabbed the phone and called Millard at work. (One of the unheralded joys of being married is always having someone to bitch to, for among a woman's most basic needs is having a complaint department that's always open.)

"The ducks are in the water lilies," I sobbed into the phone.

Millard got it right away. "Are the buds gone? The leaves? What's left?"

"Nothing," I whimpered. "Just a leaf or two."

He was silent.

"Well, you know," he said in his soothing, contemplative drawl, "I hope that the worst thing that ever happens to us in life is having ducks in our water lilies."

For the remainder of our years together, "ducks in the water lilies" became a family shorthand for anything we overreacted to.

It got used a lot.

And come July, there wasn't a single water lily in our pond. Only seven fluffy peeps.

While Millard alone doted on Cosi's evil soul, we both agreed that she was nothing less than a paragon of Jackitude, and we began to show her off at the Jack Russell Terrier trials in New York's horsey suburbs, where all the dogs seemed to be wholesome, muddy "outdoor dogs" that certainly had never had a Dairy Queen, and all their very fit owners clomped around in ancient wellies (ditto). Unquestionably, too, none of these dogs had ever slept in a bed. Plus, most had names like Jock and Tom. Mozart wasn't in it.

We discovered there were whole towns upstate, actually, where you couldn't find a horse without its attendant working Jacks, all doing what tiny terriers have traditionally been bred to do: kill rats in stables by breaking their necks.

Oh, this was one intriguing world. We'd known about Westminster, of course, the annual AKC beauty pageant at Madison Square Garden. Jack Russells were blackballed from show business back then, since basically, they were mutts. And Jack people were pretty proud of that. So they—we—held our own shows, where scores of incredibly noisy dogs competed to see who was shortest, podgiest, jauntiest, and most true to type. Not one, by the way, was ever voted Miss Congeniality.

Showbiz tyros that we were, Millard and I were convinced that Cosi was a jewel of Jackish beauty, and with Millard on the sidelines admiring us both, I trotted her around the show ring a few times. Once, she actually took a second-place ribbon. We hung it in the kitchen.

We entered her in the races, too, these hysterically funny runnings of several little dogs in mad pursuit of a lure that looked like a tail but "smelled like rabbit." Or rat.

At the end of the shortish track—these are mini-dogs, after all—great bales of hay are piled up with one Jack-size hole in the middle. The lure is dragged along the track back through the hole, and the first crazed dog to squeeze in after it, wins. Then there's some scary action on the far side of the hay bales, where fearless human volunteers in elbow-length leather gauntlets try to separate overexcited barking, snarling little spotty dogs with razor teeth, before they rip one another apart. It wasn't all just toughing it out in that pit, however. There was the occasional mild complaint when one or the other pup came away missing part of an ear.

Cosi never won that either. Usually, when the chutes opened and all the other dogs ran like hell, she'd sort of wander off the course, snuffling. She was red-ribbon pretty, our girl, but a little, and lovably, dim.

The third and most rigorous of the trials was the go-to-ground. Here, in a mown, scrubby field, the show managers had simulated a vermin hunt (so Brit) by slipping the canine contestants nose-first down a hole in the ground into a very black, very tight tunnel. To make things interesting, the organizers placed inside it a live mouse in a small cage. (How I bled for that mouse, its tiny heart pitter-pattering in the dark). Each dog entered alone; the judge had a stopwatch; and the contestant that got to the mouse fastest and barked, won. (In real life, Jacks in hot pursuit of rodents sometimes get stuck in those holes. When this happens—if they can be reached—they're pulled out by the short, docked tails that have been left just long enough for an owner to get a hand around.)

While they never said anything to us overtly, never actually snickered, Millard and I decided that, after several Saturdays at these events, the regulars, those waxed-coat men and women who docked their own dog's tails and casually employed terrified scapemice, were conveying to us, by example, how wimpy we were. So we never entered Cosi in the go-to-ground. She had merely the stub of a tail, anyway, and given the fact that we three slept in the same bed, Millard and I weren't about to teach her how to scurry down grubby holes in our garden. I wasn't much on teaching her to bring me gifts of dead vermin, either, unless they were minks. Millard, though, loved the whole manly hunt thing and so was enormously pleased when I eventually found an antique English watercolor depicting a trio of what, to our recently educated eyes, were clearly Jack Russell ratters. The frame bore a legend only mad Anglophiles could love: *Three of the Right Sort.*

❈   ❈   ❈

Cosi was adorable and fierce, but she was only human after all, and she'd begun to develop curiously human-type problems—bad breath being the most in-your-face, but hardly the strangest. The strangest was that she was going bald.

Along about the end of our first year together, I'd begun to notice black spots, like very large freckles, becoming increasingly visible on the piggy pink skin beneath her fur. As more and more pink emerged, I phoned her breeder in Texas (who, undoubtedly, like so many backyard breeders, had *never* planned on hearing from me again), only to have her swear up and down that she'd never seen such a thing on any of her dogs. Was I feeding Cosi the wrong thing? Had I traumatized her? Was she sick? (Did I have a receipt?) More to the point, was I being a rotten parent? Again?

So more usefully, I called our vet, who recommended that I take her to be examined in Manhattan, to the best animal hospital in the area—some said in the country—since she might have a thyroid issue.

A thyroid issue. That sounded dire. I tucked my balding Cosi under my arm, put her in the back of our newish station wagon with a few of what I hoped would be comforting blankets (all antiques dealers—even dormant dealers—drive station wagon–like cars with a blanket or two in the well) and left her loose behind the wire partition to enjoy an unobstructed view of passing gas station attendants. When I pulled onto the Long Island Expressway, it was a cloudless, sunny day.

To get to Manhattan from Long Island, you must travel under or over the East River. Ostensibly, the most direct route is through the Midtown Tunnel, which was then very long and very dark, with the requisite allegorical light only at its faraway end. About a minute into its maw, I noticed a definite smell in my car. I sniffed.

Potent.

Familiar.

Awful.

And I realized that Cosi had pooped hugely in the back and that I was about to be trapped in the car with it and with her lurching around in it as I maneuvered through midtown traffic.

Long afterward, I came to the conclusion that, to a little dog, when the car radio and the sun go out simultaneously, that's plainly The End of the World.

Anyone would poop.

Back then, though, I just felt sorry for myself: three useful blankets undoubtedly shot, and so much for that new-car smell.

Ultimately, though, it only reinforced my belief that she'd have been no good at all in the go-to-ground.

They never found out what was wrong, by the way, and we just got used to having an almost-hairless terrier. In truth, I grew rather fond of that rounded pink belly with its dappled black spots. Millard did, too. In fact, I'd never seen Millard love any thing or person the way he loved Cosi, balding or furred.

By today's parenting standards, Millard hadn't been much of a father, at least not in the caretaking, demonstrative sense. With the exception of their irregular weekend bondings, Barden's feeding, clothing, worrying-about, schooling, embracing and socialization had been all Mom's job. Dad did the pizza runs and bike-riding stuff, but babies and children, for some unfathomable reason, made Millard uneasy. And I was okay with that. Though if I occasionally hinted it was absolutely necessary, he *would* pick up a child. But he'd hold it gingerly, at a distance, the way you or I might hold a cute baby alligator. And I don't think I ever saw him spontaneously hug or kiss Barden, but then, he didn't hug or kiss me spontaneously, either. Though I yearned for him to.

In essence, Millard was a sweet-tempered, slightly socially inept, none-too-demonstrative man. But he always had a smile on his face and he was perpetually curious. He was also partially deaf from a childhood illness, which meant that you couldn't hope to talk to him if his back was turned, and you could never whisper. I used to kid him that if he'd ever been drafted and it was whispered from man to man along the trench that his unit should fall back, Millard would be the only hero. On the other hand, you should know that, as he aged, he was often mistaken for Harrison Ford. (We'd laugh about whether he ought to sign those autograph books or not, and it got us nice tables once or twice at Manhattan restaurants.)

Eventually, it became evident to me that he'd been saving up all his love for Cosi: so tough, so small, so undemanding, so—compared to a wife and son—complication free. He didn't begrudge me a little of her love, though, and I was allowed to love her in return. Thus, to planting gardens, restoring houses, tending ponds and Barden, we added one more mutual passion.

We'd been refining the Main Street house for ten runaway years when I got the itch again. This time, it was for a Gothic Victorian on the water a half mile away.

For me, it was key that the house was such a wreck.

What a project!

For Millard, it was key that the house was such a wreck.

What a folly!

In my favor:

It was a ruin so architecturally remarkable; so inexpensive; so on the market for months. (Of course it had been on the market for months, the broker told us much, much later. Husbands turned and fled in the driveway.) But it was so full of potential; so, well . . . pretty.

In Millard's favor:

The money we needed to buy it.

In the years since, friends have accused me of pushing a screaming and yelling Millard into buying "that wreck." Heel marks on the road and all that. But they were only partially right. Truth is, we put a deposit on the house in the fall, then spent the winter doing our semi-Socratic thing.

I'd argue the Pro:

"It's beautiful. It's romantic. It needs us. It won't be expensive, we can do it all ourselves. It needs us." And oh, there was that water. And the little carriage house. And the falling-down boathouse. And the falling-down bulkhead. And the fallen-down trees all over the (strangely squishy) lawn.

He'd argue the Con:

"I love it where we are. I'm tired of fixing up. I'm fifty. I'm old. We can't afford it. That rotten porch. That dicey slate roof. That incinerator smokestack across the harbor. Those rotting hulks by the shore. That's a view?"

Then I'd argue the Con:

"Millard, if you don't want to do this *that* much, we won't. I never want to push you into anything. We just won't."

And he'd argue the Pro:

"Carol, if you want this so much, we'll do it. I want you to be happy. We'll just do it."

All winter, we worried the thing back and forth, and every time we went to look at the house again, he'd stop talking to me for a few days. Which was hard.

Until May, when we moved in. And oddly, there wasn't that much to do.

We were both disappointed.

To prove myself to Millard, however, and to justify this totally unnecessary move, I'd decided that, workwise, I would really outdo myself. So the day after we closed, I drove over to our extremely detached garage and, from its ceiling, hauled down a very tall ladder. Up in the old kitchen (well, not really the *old* kitchen, which was actually in the basement), the plaster walls and ceiling had once been canvassed over.

Now canvas was, and still is, the traditional method for stabilizing cracked and crumbling plaster, since plaster—what with movement and settling and the passage of time—is *always* going to crack. You can patch it, you can replaster it, still, the time-honored method for *fixing* implacable plaster is covering the walls with canvas. Unfortunately, however, humidity and steam heat and continued movement cause canvas to buckle and blister and lift, so that in my new old kitchen—a lovely room with tall windows, 1940s cabinets and forest green Formica panels below the chair rail— a triangular hunk of limp old canvas was currently hanging down from a corner of the ceiling. This was the kind of thing that scared off husbands, and this was why I'd brought the ladder.

Standing on its sturdy top step, I reached up, grabbed the offending flap in both my hands, and yanked. With a satisfying *rrrip*, it pulled down and away. And as I looked at my handiwork and stretched to my right to continue on, a few small chunks of plaster fell through my hair and shattered on the floor. Then, a few more. Then, suddenly, a scrim of plaster dust materialized around me in the morning sunlight.

And I watched, the entire exposed triangle of ceiling began to break apart and fall. The whole thing was going to drop. It was about to be a disaster.

But I would save the day.

My hair powdered with white, my tongue dry with panic and grit, I fairly slid down the ladder and flew to the garage. In the old woodshed attached to the outside of its far wall, I'd noticed a longish joist. I might be able to use it as a "dead man." If I was lucky, its ten-foot length would reach both the ceiling and the floor and jam that canvas back in place. Grabbing one end of the grimy timber and struggling with its surprising weight, I maneuvered it out of the shed, through the garage, up the back stairs and, after some backings and forthings and swearings and bruisings, positioned it for entry through the kitchen door. Peering cautiously around the jamb, I could see, to my relief, that nothing more had fallen. So, holding the piece of wood like a battering ram, I entered the kitchen at an awkward trot and as swiftly as I could, eased it upright. Deftly, I caught the now-much-enlarged corner of hanging canvas with the timber's flat top and quickly slammed it into place.

Incredibly, the other end of the joist just reached the floor. I was saved.

Panting, I wiped the sweat and dust from my face with my shirttail and left the kitchen, locked the house and, much subdued, drove home.

As the day wore on though, I began to feel increasingly pleased with myself. I was competent. Capable. Resourceful, even. There was no question that I'd be able to do a good deal of work by myself; which meant that Millard would be less burdened, have less to feel responsible for, have less to complain about and less reason to be pissed with me.

So I could hardly wait to tell him about my coup. (Actually, I didn't. I called him at work.) At dinner, I described the whole scene in great detail, making it as sound as melodramatic as I've made it sound above. I was Wonder Woman. I was Sheena, Queen of the Jungle. I was Lara Croft with normal lips but older, wiser . . . and more modest. Too impatient now for Millard to finish eating, I dragged him to the car with his coffee cup in hand and sped over to the "new" place to show him what I'd done.

It tells you something about us, I suppose, that this was the kind of adventure that made Millard proud of me. In his usual nonverbal way, of course. And it tells you, too, that he expected no less of me. This had been clear from the day we met. Millard had always assumed that men and women were absolute equals. A woman could run a business, hoist a ladder, paint a house, climb a thirty-foot scaffolding, move a sofa, dig a hole. I was seventeen when we met, you'll recall, so I never knew I couldn't.

But as we parked in front of the new house that evening, it was just getting dark. In the gloaming, the house looked more ramshackle, daunting and brutally irreparable than ever and Millard's face, happy and expectant till then, went dark. He was going to stop talking to me again. Right now.

There were some twenty-five keys to this house and I kept smiling and trying to distract him as I struggled to find the right one fast enough to get him inside before he could look too long at the roof, the flaking paint, the sagging porch and on it, the stained sofa that our predecessor had left for the Salvation Army that they wouldn't take.

I got all babbly and coercive. I was selling an antique.

"C'mon, Mill. Wait till you see! Just let me get this door open." ("I know this table has a few dents and nicks and is missing most of its hardware and has three legs replaced and woodworm, but it's just what you've been looking for!" Or not.)

Finally, I found the key, and we were through the door and safely standing in the hall, and I grabbed his hand and pulled him toward the kitchen where triumphantly, I flipped on the light switch.

There was my dead man standing tall and true in the far corner.

There was the wedge of canvas, sticking to that corner like glue.

But the entire rest of the ceiling had fallen down.

And Millard loved it.

He loved being right about this money pit of a house. He loved knowing what I didn't know: that a broom and some drywall would put all to rights. And despite his inherent feminism, he loved my ineptitude. Most of all, he loved the egg on my face. In some major, mysterious way, it eased his angst AND . . . it would give him a really good story to tell on his impulsive, impossible, maladroit wife.

But to have him laugh like that every day for the rest of our lives, I'd have swept up old plaster forever.

❖   ❖   ❖

His own most challenging jobs turned out to be the mere placing of a lally column under the sagging ceiling of the garage; the putting in of hooks and screw eyes on the lower halves of those tall, warped screen doors that didn't completely close and latch; the locating and repair of the open sewage pipe (yes, sewage pipe) that had been mucking up the lawn; the carrying of some HEAVY new telephone poles down to reinforce the bulkhead—at low tide, of course, with plenty of male help; and finally, the simple installation of our new dishwasher and the repair of some plaster that had fallen from the living room ceiling because the pipes had once burst, and . . .

Hey, there we were, with nothing to do but cosmetics!

We'd never been much for new kitchens and bathrooms, anyway. We were all about moldings and clapboards, faux graining and correct wallpapers, so we didn't mind the 1955 stove or the 1915 flush-o-matic toilets—all seven of them.

Cosi took the move in stride. She weed in every room, upstairs and down, and pooped only in the rooms we hadn't started to work on yet.

Thus, finally, with the exception of the unique, dank Spring Room that housed an artesian well in the basement and seemed to be permanently under three inches of water, most of the scary repair was enough under control that we began to congratulate ourselves on our "bargain." Or rather, I congratulated ourselves. Millard never would admit to me that he loved the house. Never. Although he carried not one, but two pictures of it in his wallet, which were two more than he carried of Barden or me.

By the Fourth of July, 1986, the house was working sufficiently well that we could think of inviting his recently remarried father and stepmother for a visit. We had no air-conditioning, but we did have a million numbered screens that we hurried to hoist up before they arrived. Millard and his father were Georgia-born and never-no-minded the heat. I could be an occasional good sport, depending on the humidity. Joan, the new wife, we weren't sure about. She had been my mother's friend (bridge, not golf), and my own darling father, whom I'd lost just that spring, had once hinted to me that he wasn't so fond of Joan. This was so unlike my father that I'd remembered the comment but decided to reserve my own judgment.

They arrived on a scorching afternoon, and after the five-dollar tour, during which they tried really hard to be polite about our elderly, eccentric project, we all sat back and relaxed on our sparsely furnished wraparound porch, sipping iced drinks and admiring the egrets. Millard's father, courteous and cheerful as always, had his usual fastidious napkin wrapped around the omnipresent glass of scotch and, beaming proprietarily at his bride, good-naturedly boasted that everywhere he'd asked in Pittsburgh, he'd heard the same thing about her: "Joan was a real lady."

Oh dear.

She was something of a cipher as well: attractive, of course, slim, pleasant, sure of herself, but with an abrasive Pittsburgh accent (e.g., "hoss" instead of "house," and "dahn tahun," not "downtown") and little to add as we small-talked our way through the crabgrass and the heat and how much it might cost to fix up our bargain and whether we could afford it and the curiously empty house across the street, where they'd recently discovered a leaky oil tank buried in the lawn. EPA restrictions were just becoming effective then, and we'd heard that the absentee owners had been forced to spend seventy-five thousand just to dig up the old tank and put in a new one. Millard's father was appalled. As the gorgeous light of what one of our sniffier friends once referred to as our "vulgar sunset" flickered to dusk in the west, Millard and I made up our minds that the next day—if it was all right with our houseguests—we'd take half an hour or so to run over to the empty house to learn what we could about oily lawns. We were worried. If a contemporary house could have oil tank trouble, imagine what *we* might be in for.

Also, after only a day, we were anxious to be by ourselves.

So late the next afternoon, leaving careful instructions with Joan to hook the screen door high and low so Cosi couldn't get out, we walked across the street.

You know what's coming.

As Millard and I kneeled side by side, examining a telltale patch of blackened grass in the late-day sun, there was a terrific *bang* on the street. A hedge hid our view, but someone was screaming out there, and people were yelling. Millard stood up and ran to see.

I stood up, too. Sunstruck. My mind ice white.

Only the upper catch of the screen door had been hooked, you see, so that Cosi had gotten out the bottom, where it opened just enough to let an insufficiently plump little dog squeeze through in search of her people (why hadn't we gone for ice cream more?); onto the porch, down the steps, up the driveway and across the street; a gutsy little dog who had never crossed a street, never been out on a street and never been left in the care of anyone who didn't understand that one could want to kiss a dog. She was hit by a carful of kids taking a curve too fast, and they never even stopped.

Arms around each other, we found our way back into our house, where I climbed the stairs and didn't come down for two days.

Millard wrapped our Cosi in a soft old blanket and buried her where we could always see her: down a short flight of stairs at the corner of the veranda, looking toward the harbor.

And our houseguests wouldn't leave.

Not only didn't they leave, but Joan—who'd never had dogs or children—seemed determined to overlook how crushingly bereft we were. She kept smiling her smarmy lady-smile and wanting to chat and trying to get me to eat something or have a drink of water. Why do they always offer you water?

I was galled by her cheerful insensitivity.

She hadn't hooked the screen.

I never forgave her for that.

Much later, a friend, a dog lover who came to

visit and condole, told me she had never seen a man as devastated as Millard was that day.

How intense, the emotional investment we have in our dogs. Neither Millard nor I—and at that time we'd been married almost thirty years— had ever left ourselves as entirely vulnerable to each other as each of us had been to that little dog. Long marriages develop comfortable areas of opacity and restraint. And raw bits, of course. So when he left for work in the morning for the rest of that summer, I could see from the kitchen window that he was doing his best not to look at that sickening spot in the road as he swung his car out of the drive. I never mentioned it though.

For myself, I eventually took to approaching the house from the opposite direction, despite its being very much out of my way. For almost two years, I couldn't look at that curve. Then one day, I could.

Three months before Cosi died, I'd lost my beloved father. I may have told you that. He and I hadn't shared a life in decades, and his death, though unbearably wrenching, seemed an old one somehow—a death of a childhood love.

A pet's loss can't compare with human loss; yet we love our pets with such utter transparency; with joy and naïveté. That's why the love and death of dogs (and I stretch here, to include cats and ferrets and guinea pigs—but not snakes) remains forever tender. And keeps alive in us some lasting scraps of our valuable, childlike hearts.

Good dogs.

Chapter Five

Devil Dogs

Cosi was slow to leave our house. There we'd be, thinking we were over it, when we'd come across some hairy half-chewed rawhide behind a chair, or some half-chewed chair.

From the scatterings of white hairs on our blankets to the irreparably scratched vinyl in the back of the station wagon to the thin leather leash limp by the door to the occasional nugget of dried old poop, she was with us every day. Even the Dairy Queen lost its frozen luster. Not to mention sex, which wasn't fun somehow, without its customary canine soundtrack. Or was it sorrow?

Our house was as bleak as our hearts, since we'd really just moved in. Odd brooms and single work gloves and stacked cardboard boxes jammed the corners of our unused and unusable dining room-to-be and hid our kitchen counters. In the space that was meant to become the living room, scratched and scuffed wood floors were fortunately invisible beneath piles of book-filled boxes that had one further advantage: They'd been stacked high enough to prevent our having to look at sad curls of peeling paint. It would be months — actually, years — before we'd get the bookcases built in that room; the bookcases on top of which I would eventually put my enlightened yet pretentious busts of the Greek philosophers; of Mozart and Robbie Burns; before I painted the room a particularly subtle Bazooka pink; before we got our books unpacked at last, and put away.

But Cosi wasn't there, even though Millard had a nice big workshop in the basement where she'd have loved to squat. In the fifties, this had been a cool-man-cool knotty pine rec room with the requisite wet bar. Except for its being currently strewn with several sizes of drill bit, odd angles of chrome plumbing parts, a hundred thicknesses and colors of electrical wires, and unmanageable coils of scrunchy BX, it almost still was. Had we preferred recreation to grief and repair, our partying would have had to take place amid the newly dangerous gray rags of asbestos hanging from heating pipes (Millard eventually redid them with shrink-wrap) plus the brown water seeping through the otherwise picturesque rubble walls in the adjacent furnace room that had turned the rec room's strip oak floors, well—spongy. Jitterbug on sponge? Not really.

There was nothing here we couldn't handle, of course, but without the accustomed leavening of our Cosi, we felt overwhelmed. Forlorn. Depressed, actually.

It must be human nature to yearn to immediately replace some very dear thing that you've lost; or even to believe you can.

"Damn," you say to yourself. "I can't find my favorite warm scarf. I guess I'll have to go down to that department store where I found it four years ago and buy another one."

And you actually expect this exact beloved scarf—without its tattered fringe and coffee stains—to be still in production and still in stock. It's only been four years, after all.

And it's not that you'd be satisfied with a nicer scarf than the one you've lost, either. You want that familiar feel against your neck, that color for a wintry day. You want *that* scarf back. Now.

Which is what Millard and I tried to do about five months after we lost Cosi.

❖   ❖   ❖

First, though, let me confess that I would have tried to clone her in a shot, ferociousness and all. But cloning was science fiction in 1986. Had it been an option, I'd have been first in line because, as dubious as the procedure seems and doubtless is, I have vast sympathy for anyone who hopes to replace a loved one that way.

(I confess, too, that I've saved two strips of tape and a piece of gauze that they left on Millard's arm. You know, just in case.)

And while science hasn't worked out all the bugs yet, they will surely get it right someday and oh, I'd love to be around to see it. Because then, ah joy, millions upon millions of beloved dogs and husbands will rise again to complain that it's too cold to go out for a walk and where's that leftover steak?

So we started to look around for another Jack Russell puppy. Or rather, I started to look around, since, as you know by now, I was ever the designated shopper. It was the sort of job I was born for, anyhow. All those years of antiquing the East Coast, picking out what I thought I could resell, had made me good at it.

I wish I could have done things right, though: called the august American Kennel Club, for instance, which is where one would ordinarily start the search for breeder recommendations. But it didn't like "us," you remember. So I tried Texas again and discovered that, for some strange reason, Texas wasn't taking my calls. Closer to home, I heard about one Long Island breeder who didn't have a litter but was expecting one next spring. Spring?! We wouldn't last till spring.

And then, finally, I talked to someone who talked to someone who knew a breeder in England.

Wow, I loved that idea from the get-go. Our very own new puppy arriving straight from the cradle of Jacks! An Imported Dog, so to speak. Made in England. Like our china.

But here's where I went wrong.

In my haste to fill the chasm where our love-dog used to be, I didn't follow the drill. I didn't ask for pictures of the puppy's parents, didn't see a decent photo of her or her littermates or her great uncle on her dam's side.

And here's an interesting sidebar, one you may not be aware of yet.

What I've described above is exactly how,

before that mandatory "first year" is up, widows wind up marrying old family friends who seem to walk the walk and talk the talk. They're in such a grieving hurry to replace what they've lost that they forget to ask about the compulsive gambling, or the brother in Leavenworth or the wife who was "outgrown." They take the undemanding route. As do widowers, who are possibly even less discriminating, and heedlessly (disappointingly) happy to wind up with the bringer of the seventh casserole.

Which must be why, in my own urgency to stopper the hole in our hearts, I mailed off a not unreasonable sum of money to an unknown breeder in one of those picturesque-sounding shires of the UK, trusting that I'd receive, in turn, a small crate at La Guardia's freight depot bearing your typical twelve-week-old, brown-spotted Jack Russell bitch.

I began to live for that day.

Freight depot parking at La Guardia is not for the fainthearted.

On an overcast, coolish October day, just as they laughably do in the movies, I left my car right in front at the curb because there was nowhere else to park, and in the dim freight office, after much exchanging of paper and photo IDs, took avid possession of a small green plastic case randomly slapped with scarlet LIVE ANIMAL stickers. Hurrying with my treasure to my—hey!—ticketless car, I realized that amidst the paperwork and stress, I'd barely found time to peek through the door's wire grill for more than a glimpse of three or four squares of smooth white fur. Only when I put the crate on the backseat did I notice that said white fur seemed unusually quiet. She was taking this well, I decided, while I, on the other hand, wasn't. I was dying see what she looked like, not to mention dying to hold her. So several times a minute on our ride home—seriously endangering scores of fellow drivers on the LIE—I rubber-necked in hopes of catching some key body part in the rearview mirror, a bright eye, a black nose, an ear, maybe.

But I saw little and heard less.

Could this pup, who had just flown from Heathrow in the freezing belly of BOAC, be thirsty or hungry or . . . severely traumatized? Or—and here I flashed on my first days with my newborn son—was she even breathing in there? I needed to get home.

At the front door at last, I wrestled the travel crate out of the car and into the empty kitchen, closed the kitchen door ever so gently, hoping not to startle little Blue (don't ask), and breathlessly unlatched and dropped the wire door of the dog carrier. Out stepped—shaking herself and smelling really rank—a tiny, pure white terrier, the spit and image of a Chihuahua: bulging brown eyes, pointy upright ears, skinny white body on long, sticklike legs.

Yikes.

Which doesn't begin to express my misgivings.

I checked the label on the crate, but I had the right dog. And as I stared, unbelieving and unnerved, she confidently weed on the floor and explored a handy electrical socket. This non-Jack. This mutant. This pogo.

What's a pogo, you ask?

Think cat.

Though to be more precise, "pogo" is the dog aficionado's term for a pup that can—from a standing start— spring straight from the floor to the top of your dresser, say, to the top of your sofa, your kitchen countertop, to your guest's food-filled lap. Although Blue, as it soon became disappointingly apparent, wasn't having laps. She wasn't having people much at all, to be absolutely frank about it. And not to speak ill of the bitch, but if canines can have attention-deficit disorders, Blue was highly in need of meds.

Manifesting utter disinterest in Millard or me or any drop-by kids or birds or pink-tailed, be-whiskered vermin—which our new house had in spades—Blue came to us with the metabolism and attention span of a fruit fly. She was so un-Cosi, she might as well have been a Lab. And if we'd been thinking at all, she should have been. Although to be honest, Labs have always been much too popular for me. In common with certain nameless German cars you see everywhere in certain nameless suburbs, Labs are like fleas on a dog. Personally, I like the odd. The Georgian named Millard. The falling-down house. The Humber (I'd now worn out four). The suit-wearing child.

This Jack Russell/Chihuahua/fruit fly dog?

Well, one thing was certain: There'd be no sending her back. Even if we wanted to, we couldn't easily overlook what transatlantic horrors the poor little thing may have undergone that had turned her overnight from a Jack Russell terrier into—could dogs transmogrify?—a This. This sui generis Blue. She didn't want to be with us, or snuggle with us, and she didn't care when we got home or went out. Alone in our kitchen, she busied herself with creatively chewing the muntins around the glass in the kitchen door and when she tired of that, the cookbooks on the counter. (Most dogs like books, you know: It's their spines—all that animal glue. Though most dogs have natural good taste as well, and therefore like books.)

And in case you're wondering why she was loose in our kitchen munching books, all the foregoing took place before that lovely wire crate with the little fleece on the floor became the training method of choice. And by the way, Blue wasn't eating that door in hope of escape. She just had a mad passion for aged wood with lead paint sauce. Unfortunately for her (as I've come to appreciate lately) we had plenty to gnaw. But little by little, as I got used to Blue's appearance and disposition and tried very hard to accommodate those few of her peculiarities that were either likable or nondestructive, it hit me like a brick one day. Her English breeder had taken big-time advantage of our purported American naïveté as well as our distance from wherever she lived in Oddogshire to ship us—not merely the runt of the litter but her single unsalable pup.

Had we been had?

We missed our Cosi even more.

Though we tried to make the best of Blue. We'd always been inveterate glass-half-fools.

❁   ❁   ❁

Time drifted by, maybe even another year, during which we made genuine and satisfying progress on the house. We patched and cleaned and waxed the wood floors, cut down dead trees, stopped that seepage in the basement (cleaned the gutters!) and hired a weirdly suited-up exterminator to take a beehive out of our attic; a beehive that was unquestionably, the fellow reported to us with some pride, the largest hive he'd ever seen in any inhabited living quarters. Some fifty pounds, as I recall (about the weight of a year-old bear). When he left, I spent the afternoon cleaning gobbets of lovely sticky honeycomb off the attic floor, shoveling them into black trash bags and washing the old pine boards. I adore honey and would have eaten all those remnants on the spot had they not been studded with hundreds of dead, poisoned bees.

Now that the honeybee is in dire straits, of course I'm filled with retroactive remorse. Should we have smoked the hive and carried it outside? Should we have left it to flourish and sealed off that room? Should we have put on veiled hats and elasticized suits and become beekeepers? Should we have lived in a buzz of mutual amity? Will I ever do right by Mother Nature?

❊   ❊   ❊

Although our house had been constructed in the early 1860s, we discovered photos taken in the 1880s, and poring over these, we were able to begin, slowly, to return bits of the structure to what each once looked like. Hand-chamfered wood railings replaced wrought iron on the porches. We'd already returned the decorative open spandrels to the upper corners of the porch roof supports when we belatedly discovered these were beloved of barn swallows, which may have been why they'd been boarded up to begin with. We even installed a reproduction of the old roof cresting. A kind of "icing" around the top of our house, this was basically an architectural fillip, but terrifying to install. Millard had cleverly re-created it by first making a casting of a segment we'd found at a flea market and then, at his plant, reproducing eighty or so feet in aluminum. We were starting to have fun.

One day, through the careful research and good offices of a neighboring preservation buff (which we were inadvertently becoming ourselves), we discovered that a rendering of our house had once appeared in the 1860s equivalent of a design magazine, and in the text accompanying its proud architect's own engraving of his vision, he'd set out his hopes for how the interior might be finished.

If his creation had *ever* looked that way, it utterly didn't now, but preservationists that we were and following his directions, we tried our best to finish his house for him. We painted the faux stone walls in the hall. Millard held the straight edge and I painted, though we quickly discovered that I lacked his steady hand. So I held the straightedge and Millard painted. (And that's why a good one-third of the front hall's "stones" looked hand-hewn while two-thirds looked machined.) I spent weeks on the faux-grained woodwork, making a point of continuing the whole onto the second floor, because I'd read somewhere that most graining was confined to main floors because the majority of nineteenth-century homeowners couldn't afford to have all of the house grained. I didn't want anyone to think we were only about show (and with DIY, after all, we could be big spenders).

In period-speak, we "gussied our house up." And we did it all ourselves.

Except for the hall tile. We didn't lay tile.

And then we made a marvelous discovery.

I was still addicted to reading the antiques trade papers, and one dull winter evening, stretched out on the living room floor, leafing through page after page of gray text and grainy ads, I came across an arresting full-page photo; an advertisement for a cast-iron birdhouse that looked, gee, very much like our house. The porches were in strange places and there seemed to be a bay window where we didn't have a bay, but still . . .

"Mill, take a look at this," I said, sticking the paper under his pipe.

My spatial relations had always been a running joke between us, but Millard snapped to attention.

"That's our house! It's definitely a miniature of our house." He was really excited. "Call the dealer. See if we can buy it!"

He actually wanted to buy something! He was so excited he spilled pipe ash down his sweater and burned a(nother) hole.

I called immediately but was disappointed. We were too late. The dealer had sold the little cast-iron birdhouse almost immediately to another dealer. (Which, in case you didn't know, is how the antiques world stays afloat.) Still, after I'd confided my improbable tale to him, and perhaps, because this particular dealer was one I'd known for years, he tried to buy it back for me.

And whaddya know? He did.

Which was how we came to own a cast-iron miniature of our own house—labeled by its maker and dated 1868. Not only that, but it appeared that we'd been making a nest for ourselves in perhaps the only extant piece of residential architecture in the United States with a signed and dated birdhouse in its likeness. Over time, for those who inquired, we invented the following romantic, almost-plausible backstory:

Mr. Miller, a cast-iron maker in Providence who had until quite recently been engaged in making cannon for the North, was reading a shelter magazine in his foundry one day (I did say "almost") when he turned the page and came across architect Frederick S. Copley's engraved illustration of his "Model Suburban Cottage: In The Old English Or Modern Gothic Style." And the enterprising Mr. Miller, who'd been looking around for some way to salvage the fortunes of his moribund cast-iron factory, said to himself, "Now wouldn't that make a handsome, salable birdhouse?"

He had a nose for the birdhouse business, did Mr. Miller, because he seems to have done quite well making multiples of our house, along with a number of other, perhaps not so successful, houses. At the Rhode Island School of Design, we found a Miller Iron Company catalog from which we learned that our house was the most costly model the company offered. New and painted white, it sold for ten dollars. Had automobiles been around then, it might have been "the Caddy of the line."

Unfortunately, however, because it wasn't actually possible for Mr. Miller to see the rear of the house in the engraving, he got that part wrong. And later, when the traffic increased on our nearby road, one of our predecessors moved two of the porches, so we no longer matched the picture in the book. Clearly, though, it was our house.

We never put our "own" birdhouse outside; we kept it indoors, safe from entropic rust and the depredations of Nature. But we did find another of the Miller birdhouses to put on a pole in the garden. You wouldn't imagine that birds would actually want to live in a cast-iron house (hot!), but every spring, modest brown house sparrows nested in ours.

Meanwhile, though Millard and I were ashamed to admit it, Blue was increasingly turning out to be an unsatisfactory Cosi. After a mildly searching review of our consciences and hearts and an exercise involving some convoluted logic I don't care to recall, I arrived at the skewed but gratifying conclusion that since we only had a half–Jack Russell, a second Jack Russell would give us the whole, ideal dog. No, we'd never had two dogs before, I explained to my objecting-as-usual husband. But they were small. And two couldn't be any more trouble than one.

(We'll let that lie there for a bit.)

Besides, if Blue couldn't find a soft spot in her peculiar little heart for humans, maybe something with fur could seduce her. And maybe, too, a little friend to play with and tussle with and chase balls with might distract her from the woodwork.

Which is how Billy the Jack came into our lives: a walking, eating, yawning example of the hair of the dog that bit you.

Following the usual half-baked modus operandi with which you'll now be more or less familiar, I did a good bit of reading about the owning of two dogs. I was no longer borrowing dog books from the library, it will interest you mildly to know. I had gone pure hard-core and was buying my dog books now. Some arrived in plain brown wrappers from England, because my addiction had become too pressing, too immoderate and too often occurring on weekends or after midnight, when the library was closed.

That's where I'd read in my now well-thumbed *Raising Jack Russell Terriers* that the key thing is, even if your female has been spayed (Blue had), it's almost never recommended that you put two bitches together, basically because nothing is as vicious to a bitch as another bitch, as everyone who watches reality TV already knows.

Impatient as usual, I scouted out a litter that had a boy: nearer by this time, only in Connecticut. The pups in this litter were broken-coated Jacks, i.e., dogs with rough or curly coats. To my mind, these weren't as caressable as the smooth coats, but in their fuzzy-wuzzy way, they were cute. And Billy, with his curly white coat and brown-encircled eye, was a sweetie. From the get-go, he was this docile little ball of fur that was happy to eat and sleep and little else. For as long as he was with us, actually, Billy didn't do much but eat, sleep and grow rotund. Very rotund.

He was also a champion yawner.

Blue seemed okay with her new roommate, although I wouldn't say she welcomed Billy, or that she and Billy even liked each other, which made me sad. Because when it had first occurred to me to get a second dog, I'd had fond imaginings of the two of them curled around each other in a (tartan, perhaps?) dog bed. You know, like in the puppy calendars? But without the little bows and hats? Mostly, however, they ignored each other: Blue spending days standing on the sofa back, idly chewing on a particularly pricey gimp while keeping one eye on the squirrels out the window; Billy lying hopefully under the kitchen table, waiting for the escaped grape or the errant chip of toast. At dinner he ate twice as much as Blue, though as he grew from puppyhood to adulthood, from pudgy to portly, Billy snuffled around our table less, being happy just to lie on his bed and yawn. Eventually, I came to see Billy as the canine equivalent of some elderly member of an Edwardian gentlemen's club.

But he liked us, at least, for which we were pitifully grateful. Billy thought our laps were nice warm beds; beds that were a little too prone to sudden disappearances to suit him, maybe desireable but all the same. Not laps of the gods, for sure. Not even laps of extraordinarily important buds/owners/pals. But useful and handy and his.

Which is not to say that either of our Jacks didn't love having his/her ears scratched or, at least once a day, come nosing around for one of my inimitable tushie rubs. It was those tushie rubs that started it all, in fact. For one night, as Millard and I and the dogs lolled together in front of the television, we got a lesson on the Animal in animals.

Billy was about eight months old, which meant he'd begun to cock his leg to pee, and had we not made him a eunuch (forgive us, waxed-coat guys), he might have felt stirrings toward Blue. Well, maybe not Blue, who was always a little weirdly androgynous, but other, girlier dogs. Besides, Blue had been living with us longer and was aggressively top dog—although an arthritic field mouse might have topped our plump and mellow Bill. Despite his being such a walkover, Blue took evident pleasure in lording it over him. She ate his food, went first out the door or down the stairs (a major canine status thing), and if Billy found some neat doggy prize to investigate and Blue showed up, he'd drop his ears, tuck his tail and pad away.

On the evening of our epiphany, Blue was allowing me to share her cushion on the sofa and Billy was stretched on the floor at my feet when idly, I began to rub his tush. Billy had just sighed and yawned hugely and stood up and stretched some more, and leaned his paws against the cushion to give me a better angle, when, with a heart-stopping screech, Blue launched herself upon him.

Now, Millard and I lived a gentle, quiet life. Literally. We were soft-spoken. Lovers of classical music. (One of us, anyway.) We weren't door slammers or pot clatterers or dish throwers and we never, ever yelled in anger.

Well, hardly ever.

So you can imagine how the yelps, growls and snarls of a dogfight shocked us. Galvanized us, in fact, and we were up off our butts in seconds, staring down appalled at a shrieking tangle of teeth, limbs and fur. Billy, in his newfound maturity, was—incredibly—fighting back. He was howling, too—obviously in agony—as Blue swarmed all over him, slashing at his sides with bared, sharp teeth and screaming mean. We'd never seen a real dogfight (though I belatedly flashed on those elbow-length gloves at the terrier races), and we stood there, momentarily stunned.

But then Billy was on his back, and Blue was going for his throat. So Millard reached down to separate them—and stood up, bewildered, to see a stream of blood pouring down the arm to which Blue was attached.

Omigod.

I tore the snarling dog off his arm and threw her on the sofa as Millard clutched his forearm and ran for the kitchen sink. I looked around for Billy and saw, strangely, no blood on him anywhere. He was sitting on his quivering haunches and crying and whimpering and licking at his astonishing, unblemished fur.

Dogs and bitches didn't fight?

Well, that was why I hadn't read the How to Break Up the Dogfight parts, and why I didn't know you're *never* supposed to try to separate them. You're supposed to throw water on them.

Yup. You know, run to the kitchen—rummage around under the sink till you find a big pot—wait while it fills up (hot or cold?), run back to the fight site without spilling any, and dump.

And you know those dog book authors. Never a word about your newly refinished floors.

Fifteen stitches later, my husband and I sat alone in our bedroom and talked. We were rattled. Shaken. Hours had elapsed since the fight and the dogs were sleeping peacefully in separate rooms, but my heart was thundering in my chest at just the recollection of the thing. Wimps that we'd accepted we were, the ferocity of the set-to had terrified us. A dogfight in our house? That is *not* why one has dogs. Not me, anyway. Not us.

"It was jealousy, of course," I began. "Which means," Millard continued, "that from now on, we'll have to watch everything: which dog is where and which dog gets what." We gazed at each other in perplexity and surmise. (And yes, I'm aware of the fact that the *real* Dog People, the ones who run those terrier trials and judge Westminster, take the occasional dogfight with a grain of salt and maybe a shot or two of Johnnie Walker Red. They also attend multiple births, deal with — god forbid — dead puppies, raise packs of unmanageable "outdoor" dogs and are as emotionally invested in them, in all likelihood, as Mongolian goatherds.)

Suburban pet owners like us, on the other hand, didn't deal well with the Animal. We were all about anthropomorphizing the furry things we lived with and cared for, and even the furless things sometimes, like the whales and the manatees and the penguins. But any dog that was going to live with Millard and me, that was going to go out for a Frisbee, that was going to share the idyll of our tranquil, untroubled, restorative house, had better not fight.

Early next morning, I got on the phone and called the Connecticut Jack Russell breeder for advice, and for the first time — it wouldn't be the last — heard the politely expressed suggestion that I might not have the right personality for the breed.

"You know, Carol," she began, "I don't quite know how to say this, but some people just aren't right for our terriers. They're peppery and tough.

They need a lot of space to run in so they can tire themselves out and work off some of that extra energy. Do you have a lot of space for them to run?"

Well, we did, but the electric fence we'd put in after Cosi died kept being compromised by our happy and endless gardening. (In other words, we kept cutting those underground wires.)

"We do have space, but they don't run much," I replied sheepishly, smarting at the suggestion that I wasn't up to owning a Jack. That we weren't two of "the right sort."

"The Dog is the Dog," she offered. Politely.

And since the problem could never be the Dog, it must be us. Most likely, me.

"Thanks for your help," I said.

"Anytime," she offered. "Call anytime."

Yeah.

Well I wasn't planning on giving up my garden. And wasn't going to give up on petting one dog for the rest of our Jack Russells' natural lives (something like fifteen years.) So reluctantly, I began the hardhearted process of adopting Blue out. Billy, the more normal dog, the milder dog— and all right, the better-looking dog—we opted to keep.

And, reader, it wasn't at all hard to give Blue

away, because who doesn't want a free Jack Russell? Even a peculiar one.

You'll be pleased to know that I found a nice home for her, with children and a fenced-in yard and no other pets. I hoped, for her sake, there was plenty of historic wood in her new digs and hoped she'd find someone, someday, to love. But you know what? As we watched that car drive away, she never looked back once.

Neither did we.

Chapter Six

Dog Star

Bloodied now, we needed to fall back and rede-
ploy.

It wasn't that I'd secretly come to agree with the
judgmental breeder who'd suggested we weren't
cut out for Jack Russells. We were hanging on
to Billy after all, who seemed disconcertingly un-
moved by the disappearance of his tormentor.
Somehow I'd assumed he'd become an altogether
different dog without Blue around. Slim down
some; perk up; do a little stand-up, maybe. But
Billy remained bland, epicurean. He appeared in
my dreams, sometimes, as George IV.

I wasn't giving up on "pets" instead of "pet,"
either, because I'd kind of liked that two-dog
life. One warming dog per lap still seemed cozier

and homier than passing one fur ball from lap to lap. So it wasn't too long afterward that I sortied out to find Billy a gentler, kinder companion—a butterscotch-colored Norfolk terrier—still a terrier, and still a bitch. Merely in gender though, now.

We called her Emma, because there was something sweet and old-fashioned about her face and sturdy little body that made our mouths want to be filled with *mmmm*s.

But before we could bring our confection home for excessive spoiling and fussing over, I heard from her breeder—an international terrier powerhouse who showed her Norfolks at Westminster and who, shockingly, actually lived nearby—that Millard and I would be expected to submit to her version of a college admissions interview. She informed me that she thought she could find time to see us one weekend afternoon three weeks hence.

Be interviewed for a dog?

The scary breeder made clear to me that while Emma wasn't quite dog show royalty (she was a "pet quality" puppy; we never learned why), she was very closely *related* to royalty, so we were going to be subjected to a thorough Q and A to establish, basically, whether we were good enough for the dog. Given my history, I was justifiably nervous. That, and the fact that the woman's kennels were cleaner than my house.

But in those splendid kennels we got to meet Emma's relatives and siblings for a change, and a handsome bunch they were, all blocky and cinnamon and bursting with feist. Though I found myself thinking . . . "Wait, offspring seldom look like their parents." (Ours didn't. Did yours?) And they can't actually be counted on to inherit the choicest parental traits. Oh, all right, there are your occasional Mozarts, father and son, and a Bach or two or twenty, but I neither look nor behave like my mother, I think (though any success I've had in that department took years of concerted effort). But what about Einstein's children? Or Tolstoy's? Or Michelangelo's? (I know. Yes, I know.) Why, exactly, should meeting parents and sibs relieve anyone's anxious heart? Yet, the obsessive tracing of bloodlines seems to be of vital import to those who follow horse racing, for instance, or British sovereigns, or the breeding of dogs. And I suppose *that's* because line breeding, inbreeding and outbreeding outcomes are easier to analyze and correctly predict than the stock market, say. Because you always know just where to lay the blame for those prick ears or that Hapsburg lip.

❧   ❧   ❧

Eventually, after an hour-and-forty-five-minute grilling, we were qualified as Emma-worthy and presented with our darling little pup. Plus an eight-page listing of vitamins, of vets suitable for vetting Norfolks (only one or two in all of Long Island, naturally), dog groomers with the proper training (because the breed must be "stripped," not cut) and several brands of prohibitively expensive dog food. Conveniently missing was the page on housebreaking.

Housebreaking requires focus and commitment, and we'd only tried *any* kind of formal training once before, with Cosi, who *was* housebroken if you got her out the door on time. But in those days, this was far from our major problem. That was Cosi's temper. And for that small failing specifically, we'd been put in touch with an "aggression specialist"; a well-recommended teacher and dog expert who'd devoted himself solely to "humane" dog training.

When, with relief and childlike hope, we'd opened our door to him back then, Cosi had taken one look at his copious facial hair (second only in her tiny mind to a Texaco uniform) and made for his ankles. After a rough fifteen minutes, toward the end of which we finally got a leash on her, the three of us hurried outdoors for her introductory "training walk"—if you can call the guy's non-stop dancing away from an enraged little terrier "walking." I think it was then that he became very afraid, because our paragon of compassion wound up "hanging" Cosi from her leash.

Not part of any dog training manual I'd ever read, and none too "humane" to boot. And that was the end of that.

But so . . . housebreaking. We seemed never to have acquired the knack.

And curiously, while the famous Norfolk breeder's dogs had tidily modern living quarters outdoors in impeccable kennels, her house smelled distinctly of pee. Shortly afterward, so did ours.

Somewhere in between Billy and Blue, I'd begun to write about antiques and design, and with my ill-gotten gains—ill-gotten because I would have written (ungrammatically, if admissibly) "for free"—I began adding loving touches to our Ph.D. thesis of a historic house: a fitted carpet woven from original nineteenth-century point-papers, for example; several needlepoint Gothic chairs; a silk-covered settee. Need I limn the irregular yellow stains on them all?

Thankfully, however, Emma wasn't evil with Billy, and everything might have been tickety-boo if it weren't for the fact that—with Billy having grown completely into his, albeit compromised, dogness—he suddenly felt compelled to lift his leg on top of Emma's pee. Sometimes, on top of Emma. She didn't "make" much, of course, but she made it in every part of every room, so Billy's growing insistence on primacy resulted in my having to do much careful reading of the fine print on labels of stain-remover products and eventually to the reluctant purchase of a few mildly electrified plastic mats. Then, just when we were sure we'd got it all nailed down—our very own version of the time-honored family of Mom and Dad, one boy and one girl and a lot of plastic mats—Billy turned up with some very bad manners that he'd certainly learned from Blue.

Now as dogs go, Billy was small. But he was bigger than Emma. And he began by bullying her. Taking her food and growling when she tried to come near; scrapping with her over a little squeaky lamb and who was going to sit on a particularly comfy chair and who was going to eat not just his own delicious cookie but someone else's as well. Just like kids . . . with fewer inhibitions and many more teeth. How had laid-back Billy become King Kong? What was wrong (once more) with us?

But that's how we came to own our first crate.

Are there hymns in praise of the dog crate? Are there paeans? Sonnets? Doggerel?

Then I'm forced to resort to cliché: "Where have you been all my life?"

Tippy. Fluffy. Cosi. They'd all been in need of the crate. Oh god, *I'd* needed the crate.

And yes, I know what "crate" sounds like. Like pet abuse and Sing Sing. But a dog's crate is its playpen.

Really.

Because if the thing is well-equipped, with a knurly white fleece for curling up on and plenty of toys and water, and if it's big and airy and put in a room where everyone lives, well, dogs will love their crates. They're cozy there, in little nests, all enclosed and so secure; their den, if you will, like a wolf's. PLUS, it's the best of all "housebreaking" aids, because amazingly, when you leave a crated dog at home while you go out to eat or play, the safety of your furniture, woodwork, and carpets, along with your shoes, used Kleenexes, mail, mattresses and underpants is 100-percent guaranteed.

What we got our first crate for, however, wasn't actually housebreaking. It was to protect Emma from Billy, who seemed shockingly ready to hurt her. Or at least, after our recent brush with Nature, we were fearful of his intent. Millard and I had accepted the fact that we would never make good vets. We were very bad with animals-and-blood. Even worse than we were with people-and-blood. And while it may well be that dogs and bitches won't fight to the death, we took great comfort in knowing that this crate, this wonderful crate, was preventing any and all near-death experiences.

Much, much later, when I'd read many more books and watched too much cable TV, I realized that the two terriers were establishing who was going to be the Alpha Dog. Every family has one, of course. Even families with no pets. Humans don't often get so physical about things, though, and it was the physical that scared us. So we kept innocent, dumped-on little Emma crated when Billy was in the kitchen, hoping he'd get used to her "behind bars," so to speak, where he couldn't get at her. And we wondered — Is it her scent? The smell of her urine? Her uncomplicated, frolicsome self? Or was this just the canine version of sort-of-sibling rivalry that would work itself out and they'd wind up on that Thurber dog's shrink couch someday, blaming it all on me?

Belatedly, I'd begun to realize how peoplelike dogs are. How each has its own personality.

Like us, each dog is born with its own temperament and preferences. Some like watermelon. Some like carrots. (Some actually like kibble.) Some are gay. Some couldn't care less about gender. Or humans (see: Blue). Some will mourn a lifetime at their owners' graves. Some dogs want to work as hunters or herders or ratters, while others want only to snarf down liver snaps and lie around in the sun (see: Billy). Some—shall I say it?—eat poop. Some drive you crazy. Some you just love. All drive you crazy. All you just love.

And it was true that Millard had a thing for scrappy dogs, but he also grew faint at the sight of a syringe and was really, really bad with blood. Even fake Halloween blood. So one thing was sure. We really, really weren't going to spend a chunk of our lives monitoring gladiatorial terriers and our own adrenaline levels. And that's why, when poor Emma had been living in the crate for close to two months off and on, and when Billy showed no signs of liking her one jot better, we sat down for our second serious dog talk, the upshot of which was:

Reader, we divorced him.

Or less literarily, I found a nice new home for Billy with responsible people (I had recently, you'll recall, a memorable lesson in owner-interview technique).

If I sound flip, it's possibly because all this was very painful, and that's sometimes how I manage painful. We had just given up on Blue. And now we had failed again. I'd proved beyond a doubt, once more, that I wasn't very good at caring. So I wasn't feeling at all good about myself when we once more became the less-stressed owners of an only dog.

I think I hear you out there muttering that I hadn't tried hard enough with Blue; that I could have worked with Billy; that I give up too easily in general; that I have no stick-to-itiveness (Ah, mother—did you make that word up?); that I overreact to confrontations; that I'm too girly and generally, a coward.

You're probably right.

But it was us and Emma now. Emma on the bed, Emma on the lawn, Emma on my shoulder,

Emma on my lap, Emma being sick in the car, Emma being sick on the carpet, Emma refusing to chase a ball, Emma refusing to relinquish the remains of a noisome chipmunk, Emma rolling in rabbit poop/squirrel poop/fox poop . . . none of which we'd known were on our lawn and all of which we knew were on the body of this small dear dog with whom we shared a bed. So . . . Emma in the kitchen sink. Emma wrapped in towels. Emma, bathed and clean and warm. Emma.

Tearing around the lawn, chasing birds and butterflies and sniffing rancid rodent poop, Emma kept us company while we gardened in the sun. Till at some point, when our heads were safely down, she'd cautiously work her way along the lawn to the far corner of the house, where—stealthily—she'd edge around the big spirea bush and take off as fast as her runty little legs could carry her. Out of the corner of my eye I'd catch the flick of her disappearing tail, and Millard and I would have a bickery moment about who hadn't been paying attention before running like mad to get her. We never got over our fear of the road.

Though Emma was becoming more my dog than Millard's, perhaps for the simple reason that I was at home more now. Writing, by some lucky fluke, had turned into a second career for me. (Despite which, I sometimes can't resist the satisfying cliché. Though, really, what *is* a fluke?) And when I was sitting at my word processor, Emma's coarse-haired body a lovely warm weight on my lap . . . how to write about heaven?

It's not at all hard to type with a dog in your lap, you know. If I owned a small dog now, I'd be doing it as I write this. And if this were a memoir — which it isn't — I'd probably wax poetic over that. Suffice it to say that there may be nothing in life so blissful as being paid to do something you love with a dog in your lap.

Monday — Sunday — Monday — Sunday. Weeks, months, years streamed past. In some two-and-a-half star forties film of our life, pages flew off the calendar on the wall. We were both over fifty now. Millard had become almost embarrassingly proud of my work (note the "almost"), bragging to strangers about me, asking random captive visitors at his plant to read my articles, even going so far as to say he wished his dragonet mother were still alive so he could show her how wrong she'd been about me.

Did I share that wish about the woman who, with relentless criticisms in letters to her son, had broken my heart while inadvertently teaching me to be kind to my own daughter-in-law? She was right about one thing, though. She'd told Millard not to marry me because I had bad teeth.

Really.

Which is why I always paid for them myself.

Not only was Millard proud of my work, but sometimes he'd even ask if he could come along when I did interviews. He'd want to come along especially when my interviews were somewhere picturesque, like Nantucket or Sag Harbor. Once, we drove out east together to a little house owned by a talented and eccentric single mother, and while all my interviewees tended to be talented and eccentric, they weren't often humble and self-supporting.

I greeted the photographer, took out my pad of paper, asked my subject to sit down, and began. Millard looked around.

"Anything here you need to have fixed?" he asked.

That interviewee told me years later that she'd assumed we three would be arbiters of the most refined taste, and here was this lovely guy just offering to repair her home. So she got up and brought out her toaster, her fan, her portable radio, her table lamps, and if she'd been able to get it in the house, she would have brought him her car. Millard "tinkered," as she put it, till my job was done. And she never forgot him. One of her few "Good Man" memories, she tells me.

I was proud of that and, in my turn, proud of his success as a manufacturer of — I know you remember the old conversation-stopper — aircraft indicator cases.

He loved to tell the story of how he came to have a business manufacturing such an arcane, not to say singular, product:

He had been running a job shop in the early years, designing and crafting aluminum "cans" for various industries. When a can was too tricky for any other metal shop to make, the big guys called Millard. Then one day he took a phone call from a sales rep at a large and important firm who asked him if his shop made "aircraft indicator cases."

"Sure we do," Millard responded instantly. "What are they?"

(Oh, all right. They're the metal containers that all those cockpit dials and beeping-light things fit into.)

❀   ❀   ❀

I was proud then, too, of his having opened a second plant in Phoenix; of his having success-fully done the single thing that, way back when he was twenty-one, he'd told me he'd always wanted to do. Make something.

He was making many complicated somethings now. Beautifully.

Meanwhile, at our increasingly magical house, on what had previously been the top of a pergola over the semicircular drive, we'd created a small platform for dining that allowed us to eat on the prow of a great ship every fine night between May and October. Metaphorically. The grass and the water and the sunset spread themselves before us, and at nine out of ten of our twilit dinners, as the swans (yes, the swans) sailed down the harbor to their nests, we'd linger over coffee and marvel at our great good luck. Though it wasn't just over the beauty of our immediate surroundings. The town had finally blown up the incinerator smoke-stack. The coast guard had dredged the scores of decaying hulks from World War II. And our once-mucky lawn had become a smooth purl of green right down to the water's edge, where pink and white roses trimmed a bulkhead that was man-fully keeping the whole from being swept out to sea. Sometimes Millard would take his fishing rod down to the harbor at dusk, and sometimes catch a sunny or two. (He'd also indulged in a used, two-person dinghy with sails, and I'd occasionally receive a chagrined phone call from some isolated spot miles up the harbor where he'd run his boat aground. He never quite developed a "feel" for the wind.)

On those mellow summer evenings after dinner, with Emma in one or the other of our laps, we'd talk softly into the firefly-lit dark about what still needed to be done in the garden and to the house. We were impressed by what we'd built. We gloated.

C: Don't you love the way the Victorian mound looks this year? It almost looks like something you'd see in a British park.

M: That one piece of the mound seems to be less full of flowers than the other. I should go out there to check. Could be the sprinkler head is stuck or the line is clogged.

C: Oh, don't go now. Stay and talk. Do you think we should clip the wisteria this weekend?

M: It'll have to come to the top of my list.

C: How come my stuff never gets to the top
     of the list? I need to see that list! Oh,
     look, the lightning bugs are coming out.

M: Don't let me forget to look at the sprin-
     kler head. It's beautiful tonight, isn't it?
     We did such a good job pruning that old
     mulberry down by the water.

C: Let's put Emma inside and walk down
     there.

And we agreed: No vacation in the wide
world could ever offer a spot more beautiful, more
serene—sweeter—than this.

Chapter Seven

Dogged

Ah, but gentle Emma seemed to be aging faster than we were. She was slower on the stairs and happier just to lie among the flowers, butterflies be damned. And while she wasn't ill, I'd already begun to have foreshadowings of loss. We'd become such slaves to this dear dog—our router of sparrows, our Hoover of crumbs—that I lived in dread of some Cosi-like wound. How had we become so invested? I began to entertain thoughts of a second dog—a backup, so to speak. Again.

Waiting for the perfect opening—after *Clear and Present Danger*, say, followed by the diner for a beer, a bowl of minestrone, a small Greek salad, a plate of steak tidbits with well-done hash browns, one overcooked green and one soggy yellow vegetable and a tall swirl of white and chocolate frozen yogurt, all for $11.99 — I broached it to Millard.

You'd be wrong if you think you know him well enough to predict his reaction. Even I didn't know him well enough.

Because he liked it!

He liked it!

Mainly because of my plan, I think.

Or the yogurt.

I have to back up now to explain that for years, I'd been longing for a greyhound. Some secret and hubristic "Diana the Huntress" complex, I suppose; something I'm sure I should apologize for. And yet . . . could there be any dog more regal, more elegant, more noble, more ancient (i.e., "antique") than the greyhound? And since I'd long ago come to accept the fact that for better or worse, for profound or shallow, an embarrassingly large part of my life was about gathering beauty to myself . . . my house, my garden, my antiques, my art, my car, my costly and endlessly new teeth . . . a greyhound would be icing on my pink-rose-covered, three-tier vanilla and black-raspberry-jam-filled canine cake.

It had been my original hope to rescue a track dog, because the unconscionable business of dog racing results in thousands of greyhounds—the losers, the raced-out, the ones with broken legs—being euthanized each year.

Yes.

That dream, however, had one major, major drawback: When smallish mammals inadvertently cross their paths, racing dogs—bred to chase a lure—are gone. They hit forty-five mph in three long strides, and there's no calling them back because nothing stops a coursing hound. No whistle, no clicker, no squeak toy, no treat. Even dogs that were losers can run like the wind. And you remember, we were still living in an antique house. And antique houses are right on the road.

I didn't think I could deal with that anxiety.

But then I learned about an exceptional breed. Well, it wasn't a "breed" exactly. Like our JRs, it was a type, a mutt. And while it *looked* like a greyhound, it wasn't. This marvel, only to be found in Great Britain, is the Lurcher. Go ahead. Laugh. Everyone does. But the name has nothing to do with staggering drunks or Boris Karloff and *Frankenstein,* but everything to do with Ireland in the Middle Ages, where the gypsies, I learned, bred the dog for stealth poaching; their Romani word for "thief" was *lur.* This legendary creature was crossbred to be as fast and quiet as a grey or other sight hound—but to be as smart, tenacious and trainable as its other parent, a collie or terrier more frequently. With always this single stipulation: The Lurcher couldn't look like a greyhound, because only the nobility could own greyhounds, and the penalties were harsh. Like death. Or both hands.

So the gypsies learned to breed dogs that were swift, silent and smart; that looked much like the dog on the side of the bus—but not.

I LOVED the idea. Except for the fact that I couldn't save a grey, it seemed best of all second-dog worlds: a greyhound-ish dog that was smart like a collie.

And why did Millard like it?

I'd sweetened the deal by telling him that I hoped to get a magazine commission to write about the Lurcher quest, which meant that my trip would be free.

And so it was.

But first, I had to track down Dale, the president of the British National Lurcher Club: a helpful, cheerful, dog-mad fellow whom I phoned in South Yorkshire to ask how I might go about finding a collie-mix pup. And I learned from Dale—but why was I surprised?—that the nearest litter would be a four-hour drive from London. That basically, if we wanted to see absolutely the only Lurcher puppies in England in that particular week in June, we'd have to take a train first to Doncaster, where we'd pick him up, our more-than-obliging guide, and be driven to the source for truly superior Lurchers in Fell View, Low Moor, Kirkby Thore, Penrith, Cumbria. Translated into East Coast-ese—though imagine translating that into East Coast-ese—we'd be traveling all the way from Long Island to almost-Maine and back . . . to pick up a mongrel.

After crossing the Atlantic.

In Great Britain, though? Big-time Romantic! The Lake District. Wordsworth. All that.

It's unimaginable, I know, but Millard and I rarely traveled at all. In addition to our having such a good time with our own house (and okay, to my panic attacks on planes), we were neither sightseers nor gourmet eaters nor hotel buffs. When we did go beyond our usual Pittsburgh or Georgia, it was inevitably for a purpose: visiting gardens, attending air shows, seeing editors. Buying a dog abroad had to be about the most purposeful thing we'd ever tried.

❊ ❊ ❊

That June, motoring toward Cumbria with the affable Lurcher man, I'm sorry to say I barely noticed the picturesque towns and spires of distant churches. I'm sure they were there, and I do have a clear memory of a *great* many sheep. Smoke white blankets of undulant sheep, in fact, and never a human at all. Which made for one endless ride. Though at long last, very deep—oh-so-deep—in this domesticated wilderness, we came to . . . well, talk about your backyard breeders. Behind a remote, quasi-modern house we found the strangest farm scape either of us had seen—even factoring in Millard's rural southern upbringing. The owner of this homestead, a lanky hairdresser-cum-poacher and his wispy, blond and equally lanky little girl, came out the front door to greet us and lead us around to a large yard bordered by ramshackle wooden sheds, each housing some unique "pet." Not just dogs, mind you, but rabbits, owls, a fox, a polecat (think ferret), and a donkey, for openers. Mixed in with this menagerie were his fifteen adult Lurchers. Well, I'm afraid I lapsed into polite but stunned "Isn't that interesting!" mode as the proud owner showed us around, and just as I was running out of smiles, fortunately, he knelt to snap the rusty hasp of one of the wooden cribs and opened a gate. Out sped an ink black greyhound. Not too big and none too clean, it was Mom, who, for a full twenty minutes, raced gleefully around the yard barking madly at the stolid donkey and us and the heady air of fell views, low moors, etc. Seven or eight of her six-week-old litter tumbled out of the crib right behind, among them my soon-to-be Juno. Had I been a more deliberative person, less impulsive, more practical, I might have noticed a little something about scruffy Mom. . . . some trace of the manic? But no, I was charmed out of my mind by it all. In any case, a person doesn't fly 3,500 miles, then drive four hours to decide she may be not so sure about Mom. In any case, can anyone walk away from a puppy, even one with a possibly crazed parent? Besides, the magazine's photographer was standing right there to snap the schmaltzy moment. So I sat myself down in the midst of those squirmy pups and let them climb all over me, laughing with nutty delight and feeling like that old Kodak ad, but dirtier . . . and very much older.

Still, how to choose? It seemed to be coming down to the all-black licky one or the dear little sleepyhead brindle, which—I'd been nicely, pointedly, and repeatedly told—was the favorite of the owner's little girl. The raincoat I'd worn had two big pockets in it, and I was all for taking both until Millard's panicky face signaled otherwise. But which? I appealed to our Lurcher guru, who took us aside and explained—with handy live models nuzzling our cuffs—that:

"Your top-notch Lurcher should be up on its toes, so to speak, not a 'flatfoot.'

She should be athletic and have a good thick coat.

She should be fast, really fast."

I put the two pups on the ground to watch them run, but they wobbled and rolled, and one progressed dopily sidewise while the other lay down to snooze. Which is no doubt why, muddy and happy and out of my depth for the only time, perhaps, in my sadly opinionated life, I left a big decision to someone else. Dale picked the brindle, the little girl's pet.

Aargh. I steeled myself. After all, how much do you sell your daughter's pet for?

The tall breeder stood silent in front of us, seemingly focused on the sheep-strewn hills and considering, possibly, his dear little girl, the length of the trip from London, our obvious intention to buy, our (possibly costly?) pseudo-Brit clothes, our patent American-ness, and I inwardly shut my eyes.

"Well, you know," he began, in that tortured Northern accent (see *The History Boys* and *Billy*

Elliott), "she's my Margaret's favorite, so we won't want to give her away. Still, it hardly seems right to sell an untrained dog." He frowned and looked hesitantly Millard's way.

"Does one hundred twenty pounds seem too much?"

I gasped.

Oh, not *enough*! Emma had cost . . . well, you don't want to know what Emma cost. A trio of root canals for me, to start. (And if it were my habit to descend to punning, I might ask if that's why they call them canines. But it isn't.) Yet I might go on to remind you that entry fees at Westminster, and dog kennels with hot tubs come dear. Very dear.

Millard and I agreed to offer him more money, both in the spirit of fair play and the hope of leaving one British poacher/hairdresser with a better opinion of Yanks than he'd had going in. Although come to think of it, we might have left him thinking that Yanks were as naïve and spendthrift as they'd be saying at the local pub. Although on the other hand, all the way up there in Fell View, Low Moor, Kirkby Thore, Penrith, Cumbria, England, could be they hadn't heard of Yanks.

On the other hand, could be the whole "daughter" thing was a setup.

❁   ❁   ❁

Very late that night, we returned to our cozy London hotel with Juno in our prepurchased Harrod's travel crate as big as a small sports car, and the next day, when they offered to feed and water her while we went out, I developed a serious crush on London doormen. Who doesn't love a puppy, after all? Who doesn't love Brits?

Emma didn't.

Though at least she didn't get physical about it.

You may have noticed somewhere in the above that we'd gone to girl-with-girl. Toward the end, you see, Billy had truly scared me. Scared me to the extent that the dreaded two-bitch combo had grown to have actual appeal. After all, if both animals were spayed, what could they find to fight over? Other dogs? Hurtful gossip? Men?

Well, love, of course. But everyone fights over love.

And we would be ever so fair. (Forgive me. I pick up attractive speech patterns easily.) Then too, since both my dogs were of English ancestry, on the flight back with Juno I'd begun to imagine a Virginia and Vita thing. Nothing physical, of course. Just soul mates. Or possibly, given the fact that both were expats now (and Emma had added poundage as she'd aged,) a Gertrude and

Alice thing. To my baffled dismay, however, gentle
Emma hadn't taken more than a sniff of Juno before deciding that she loathed her.

And Emma never changed her mind or learned
to like her even a little. Neither, actually, did any
of the other dogs that ever lived with Juno. It was
as if she'd been born with an alien scent.

Citronella, maybe?

Cat?

But okay, Juno *was* a little weird. If you
touched a paw, she'd shriek and leap away. If you
stood up to answer the phone, she'd yip and jump
up, too. She was the most hyper dog we'd ever
owned, and I assumed it was because—though
I'd hoped for a greyhoundlike Lurcher and Juno
was three-quarters greyhound—she'd taken after
Dad, the border collie. Or—and I'm still suspicious about this—strange things happen to nice
little dogs in the bellies of airplanes.

I'm a cinephile, perhaps you've gathered, and I
refer you now to the deathless film *Babe*. Remember those pig-disdainful but articulate and clever
sheepherding dogs? The dogs dear Babe so longed
to be? Those were border collies. And our Juno—
in metabolism, smarts and shedability—was a border collie, too. Oh yes, she looked like a smallish

greyhound with a heavier coat, upstanding ears and the face of a fawn, but in her beating-too-fast little heart, she was all collie—herding us on the stairs, herding us on the lawn and herding us to the john. (Shut the bathroom door, and she'd be pacing outside when you emerged.) And Juno was the proverbial junkyard dog. She slunk. Instead of being tall and regal like the greyhound of my dreams, she grew up to be middling and skinny and slinky. And stranger yet, for the first few years we owned her, we never saw her sleep.

I mean it.

I still have the photo of the sleepy puppy she was, so I know she knew *how* to sleep, but it may have been our American air or something in our dog food or something that had occurred along the way (that plane?) that kept her continuously awake. So if she slept when we slept, we never got up early enough to catch her at it. Day and night she paced, watched, guarded.

There did come a day, though, when at last we saw her asleep—she was three or so. There on the sofa she lay, in dead-roach position: on her back, four variously bent legs in the air. Now I've read that when dogs sleep that way—exposing their bellies to the world—it means they feel utterly secure. And considering that had we not plucked

Juno from the farm, she might have spent her life poaching Cumbrian rabbits and sleeping with polecats — presumably belly down — I was thrilled to have her feel so safe.

Nevertheless, her omigod-I'm-dying shriek was hard on us.

We'd built a tidy dog run next to the house. One night, when Juno was still a small puppy and Millard was sitting outside with her for the day's final "walk," she was busily exploring the semicircular basement window well, daintily tip-toeing along its brick lip when somehow, she fell off. From the bedroom, I heard high-pitched, terrible screams and dashed out the kitchen door to find her writhing in the yard. I scooped the howling puppy up in my arms. I'd never heard a sound like that.

"Oh my god. What happened?" I shouted at a frightened Millard.

I was scared and I was mad. It would be just like him to be idly watching an airplane or lighting his pipe while some helpless pup in his care was eating a beetle or breaking a toe. I glared at him.

"I don't know. I was just sitting here, watching her, when she fell off the edge of the window well."

He tried a grin, and brushing his hand through his black hair, wiped his pipe tamp on his sock.

"She fell *in* it?"

"No. The other way. She fell on the gravel."

Fell on the gravel? That was a four-inch drop.

I put Juno down gently. She cried aloud and limped around pitiably on three legs.

Millard watched her, helplessly contrite.

"Well," I ventured, softening, "maybe it's serious. Let's get her to a vet."

At midnight, where are you going to find a vet? At the all-night veterinary hospital, naturally, about a forty-five-minute drive away.

Wrapping our precious puppy in a blanket and settling her tenderly on my lap where, motionless and limp, she continued to whimper and cry, we left Emma in charge of the house and went for an emotional late-night drive.

There's nothing quite so reassuring as the lights of an all-night hospital.

Where, in a glare of white fluorescence, we gratefully handed our puppy into the arms of a kind, concerned vet who immediately, gingerly, set Juno on the floor to gauge the severity of the trauma. I couldn't bear to look.

But Juno walked! She walked! On all four feet! A miracle!

Oh god.

It turned out she was—maybe—um, slightly bruised.

Did we want the largish bill now or should they mail it?

Did we need directions home?

Did we feel stupid?

But we were *so* relieved. The night had ended well, and we'd learned something key about our Juno. She was super-sensitive to pain and vocal about it. She was a dog who'd cry wolf.

Juno's having been born with a collie-wired brain made her a genuine working dog. And my books told me in no uncertain terms that working dogs need to work; if they don't they'll drive you crazy.

We opted for the latter at first, and because of that, she was the first dog I ever tried to train. It was sort of fun, the training. Especially the part where you lower your voice to sound like a growl. I rehearsed it in the shower. And Juno got the "sit" in a sec, but the "stay" was a metabolic impossibility. It took me a good three months to grasp that, because it seems that I don't train especially fast myself. Eventually, though, we found the perfect way to put Juno to work.

✸   ✸   ✸

Millard and I and the wonderful John Dun-leavy, a burly, green-thumbed Irishman who helped us with the heavy gardening (in his spare time, he chaired the Saint Patrick's Day Parade), had, over the years, subdued the grass leading down to the water. As our own, personal sward became prettier and smoother and freer of those open spots of sewage dating from the days when — yuck — all our toilets flushed directly into the harbor, it attracted Canada geese.

There is a large population of Canada geese in the Northeast that has never learned how to mi-grate, so each fall and spring, we'd find forty or fifty on our lawn, eating and pooping en masse. If you haven't had firsthand experience with geese and you think they're gorgeous, let me just tell you: They're dumb. Maybe all birds are dumb — even parrots. But there's no bird as stupid as the Canada goose. All alone, it justifies the extinction of its pterodactylic forebears.

After trying to run them off with the usual remedies like plastic owls and plastic snakes and evil-tasting and wildly expensive lawn sprays (oops — geese have no sense of taste) and chasing them and flapping an imaginary apron and yell-ing "Shoo," (which gets them shuffling a good foot and a half closer to the water), we fell back on our second line of defense: gimmicks. Millard had an old bullwhip, for instance, and was (sexily) adept at snapping it over their heads. Surprisingly, the crack of the sound barrier being broken scared the very stupid birds—have I mentioned they're stupid?—into gabbling excitedly and bunching up and moving a good three feet closer to the water. Trouble was, you had to walk down on the lawn to perform this singular feat effectively, and there— as I've mentioned—was lots of poop on the lawn; plus, while I practiced in secret, I wasn't, in truth, very good. So if Millard wasn't home, I was reduced to the plain old-fashioned "shoo." That's why I tried the remote-controlled toy car.

Shiny red and black with lightning bolts on its sides and a generous encrustation of plastic chrome, it was a thing of tacky beauty. With its neat remote, I intended, from the porch or even from the house, to guide that mean little robot right into our resident flock and drive it—the way cowboys drive herds, sort of—into moving on. Maybe moving away, even, because the geese seemed impressed. Or at least, they did their gabbling and bunching and shuffling thing as, on its trial runs, the car—flashing its lights and whirring insanely—zoomed toward them. This was encouraging enough that I dreamily allowed myself the vision of sitting with an iced drink while unerringly guiding my private missile toward enemy hostiles. Sort of like Cape Canaveral. Except that I'd stopped smoking, and the car, regrettably, wouldn't blow up. Equally regrettably, my missile kept getting hung up on things like tufts of persistent dandelion and the fresher clumps of poop, and ultimately, I had to relegate it to a high shelf in the workshop; graveyard of my/our failed ideas.

So at last it came to that moment when Millard and I, having tried all options short of firing off a cannon (which we'd heard was working well at local golf courses but didn't seem quite neighborly), fell back once more, regrouped, and our eye fell speculatively on Juno.

There she was, circling, leaping, trotting, pacing and basically needing to do something useful. Needing, in fact, to herd. Would she herd *anything*, we wondered, or just us? We took Juno out to the water side of the house and pointed her toward the geese. And well, to say she'd been born to chase would be an effing understatement. She LOVED chasing geese! I had merely to open the front door and whisper, *go!* and Juno would hurl herself down the stairs, race flat out across the grass and be among them, barking. Dumb as they were—have I said they were dumb?—in some dim, reptilian part of their tiny brains, they recognized our girl as the hairy threat she certainly was, and in a great flap of wings, with incensed, excited honks, they'd lift off, as one, for greener, safer shores.

I haven't mentioned that at the end of the lawn, where our bulkhead dwindled away, there was a little beachy stretch scattered with sharp stones and horseshoe crab shells and snotty strings of seaweed. One afternoon, as I sent my avenging angel off to work, the goose flock, instead of taking off for some less risky toilet, decided just to fly into the water twenty feet or so offshore, where it settled down gracefully to float and nonchalantly preen itself until the nuisance went away. Juno, revved up, heedless and possibly running too fast to stop, hurtled toward the beach and splashed in after them.

Shit! I hadn't even known she could swim!

But not only could she swim, she was a Flipper in fur. It took only seconds for her to paddle out and create minor havoc among those astonished, imbecile geese which—just as they did on land—swam two feet away and honked. With Juno hot on their tails.

Then somehow, her overexcited eye fell on a flock of mallards even farther from shore, and hey, something new to herd. She shifted objectives. She was close to a third of the way across the harbor when I began to panic.

"Juno! Juno! Come, Juno! Come, Juno!"
"Come on, good girl! Come!"
Juno didn't come.

One chilly late fall day, just months after we'd first moved in, we'd watched a yellow Lab and her pup paddle past our house and head determinedly down the harbor—our brackish harbor, with its strong currents and eight-foot tides. Millard and I were on our knees in the garden, but we thought we recognized those dogs; they lived with a neighboring duck hunter, perhaps a half mile away. What the older dog didn't see, but we did, was that her pup was tiring and falling behind. The autumnal water was icy and the two were swimming against the current. Even as we watched, the smaller dog paddled a few strokes and stopped, struggled to keep its head above water. It did, at last, but the effort cost it, and it was falling farther and farther behind. It was a game little pup, but it was failing.

We realized, just then, that the tide seemed to be carrying the two closer to our shore, and Millard and I tore down to the beach to try to drag them in before the puppy drowned. The bigger Lab, when we finally got to her, was wretched and shivering, but the little one was still, its tongue lolling out.

Bundling both of them in blankets, we drove them to their home and later, much later, phoned their owner, afraid to hear. The pup hadn't died. But it had been close.

So I watched aghast as Juno moved purposefully into the current, herding a flock that now seemed to be moving inexorably away from our shore. Damn it, why didn't they fly? And how strong a swimmer *was* our Juno. Who'd never been wet before? I was in the midst of stripping off my shoes, socks and jacket to go in after her when I remembered what a substandard swimmer I am and, forgetting my shoes, turned to run for help. And then . . . as in that classic *New Yorker* math cartoon . . . A Miracle Occurred.

Remember the sheepherding thing?

Well, somehow, even as she was paddling away, Juno was keeping an eye on the shore, and having spotted a far more important sheep getting away (me, running toward the house in nightmare-like slow motion), she turned from the ducks and began to paddle back to the beach to catch me. Bounding up the shingle and across the grass and shaking off the freezing salt water, she dashed into my arms.

❄   ❄   ❄

So that was the end of goose duty or of any practical employment for hyper Juno other than to show people how nicely she could barely "sit" (never, ever "stay") and what a superstar she was at going up for a Frisbee.

Chapter Eight

Dog People

Surprisingly, it was the nineties already, and surprisingly, we'd begun to earn more money. In honor of our newfound almost-wealth, and because I'd never been one to allow money to sit around, let alone pile up and turn into more money, I decided, among several other less defensible indulgences, to have my groceries delivered. I found a way to rationalize this luxury by telling my friends it was a lot cheaper than going to the supermarket. Cheaper, because let loose among aisles stocked with gorgeously colored boxes, shiny bottles and slithery packets all chirping "New" and "Improved" and "Drink Me," and given some even moderately inoffensive super-market music and a little air-conditioning, I could be counted on to bring home a couple of just about everything. In olden times, before supermarkets, I often had my groceries delivered because each food category came from a separate store: the butcher store, the grocery store, the bakery; plus, milk was delivered daily. At your back door. In bottles. So if you found yourself stuck at home in a third-floor apartment in a Boston suburb with a toddler and no car, you called up the butcher and the baker and ordered. On the one hand, the butcher and the baker knew you by sight and knew what grind of hamburger or type of fruit pie you liked, so you didn't really *have* to go. On the other hand, a toddler could be so numbingly boring that now and then, you just had to get out of the house.

This looks like I'm wandering, I know, but it's all leading up to Jimmy Cagney.

A new supermarket delivery man—his name was Eddie—appeared at my front door one morning. At the sound of the bell, Emma and Juno, barking the alarm, raced to see who would be first to get to the door, to the porch, to the stranger, to widdle on his shoes. It could get really hairy in those first few moments as I struggled not to open the door wide enough for them to burst through and leap upon whomever had rung while trying simultaneously to maneuver the smaller parcels into the house through the crack, smiling like crazy all the while so as not to seem like some cartoon of a suspicious, mad-dog-owning homeowner. Of course in not opening that door, I was being careful, too, because I know there are people who are afraid of dogs. For such unenlightened souls, I'd hung a small bronze plaque above the bell. "Beware of the dogs," it cautioned. In Latin. (There's a dangerous charm to living on the edge of lawsuits.)

Eddie, however, was almost as happy to see my pups as they were to see him and invited them out onto the porch where he rubbed their heads briskly, the way men do.

"I love dogs," he said, handing me my bags while Juno and Emma frantically inhaled his pants. "My wife breeds dogs."

"Oh (that explained the pants), really?" I said, politely, semi-interested. "What kind?"

"Jack Russells," Eddie replied. "Know what they are?"

"Do I know what they are? I've owned three."

"No kidding? We just had a litter. Want to see a picture?" asked Satan.

❁   ❁   ❁

And that's how Jimmy Cagney—essence and distillate of Jack—came into our lives. Tiny, rollicking, nippy, tough, barky, demanding and, oh, boy, cute, Jimmy was the embodiment of Irishness. And why we hired Norah. Or to be completely honest, *part* of why we hired Norah. The rest of the story was, well . . . I was beginning to get a little creaky. I no longer worked outdoors when the thermometer dropped below fifty, and I'd told Millard very firmly that I didn't want to carry any more furniture up the stairs while walking backward. Forward, though, was still okay. Our house was magically growing larger and larger, however, and somehow (well, of course I knew how) it was accruing much too much in the way of dustable stuff: furniture, porcelain tidbits, taxidermed birds, tiny boxes, pictures, immovable marbles and general junk. Plus, I was writing all the time. I needed household help.

Have I justified that sufficiently?

I started by contacting employment agencies and after two or three false starts, one of them sent out this small and wiry Irish angel, though I was dubious at her interview. She wasn't young. She was about my age, I guessed. (Though, what with Botox and highlights and various nips—no tucks—it had been getting increasingly difficult to know what "my age" looked like anymore.) And

Norah McNelis, who arrived at my door with short blond hair and deep (untreated) smile lines, looked to be—well, maybe not young enough for this job? Sure, she was sinewy and thin, but she didn't look like she was strong enough to run up and down our many stairs; to go out for the mail in the snow; to help me look after three hairy dogs. Three is a *lot* of dogs. But after we'd finished with the obligatory walk-through and I realized that, remarkably, she hadn't said a word about the hair-covered chairs or the hair-covered stair carpet or all those flights of stairs, and hadn't even seemed to register the millions of dustables, I was encouraged. Though still unsure. We stepped outside to sit on the porch glider and chat a little more. She was polite and somewhat stiff, and I was at my most formal and adult. (I mean, it had taken me long enough to acquire a little gravitas; I needed to take it out and dust it off every now and then.) All this time, I'd been carrying baby Jimmy Cagney to keep him out from underfoot, and I plopped him on my lap as we talked.

"Do you think you can handle this job, Norah?"

Norah had that divine Kerry accent, which I won't try to do phonetically. She might get mad.

"Well, I do think I can handle it, but," she said, and here, she reached for my squishy Jimmy

Cagney pup, lifted him out of my arms and held him up to look him in the eye, "the best thing about this job is the dogs."

And that was that.

Millard and I were turning into semi–Dog People by default. We'd never assist at a whelping or dock a tail, and I can't say I ever quite got the hang of plucking out Emma's dead hair ("stripping"), but by my reckoning, Dog People is what you automatically become when you own three or more dogs. That un-looked-for achievement, plus my now almost-lifetime of experience, had led me to believe I knew a little about how dogs think. I could tell, for example, when they were anxious about something strange (one forefoot in the air), unless they were anxious about an approaching thunderstorm, in which case there'd be pacing, wandering from room to room, trembling, whining and trying to hide under a table. I could tell when the dogs were happy, because they'd blink their eyes slowly and pant slightly and stretch their lips into a gummy "smile." I liked—and still like—to catch them dreaming. Their muffled yips alert me to their dreams, along with that faint running movement of their paws. Though I worry as I watch. Are they chasing or being chased? I hope they're chasing.

I'd gotten quite comfortable, too, with the fact that when they were licking my hand, it was either because I'd been sweating or because I'd recently handled something tasty—not because they loved me. (Juno, though, has always licked twice for a head scratch.) It's never failed to surprise me that all my dogs have understood the various names I've given them beyond their formal names; that I actually got a response to calls for Deeviedog, and Julioollio and Jujypuss, and way back there, Balooneyyooney. And I like to watch them watching me. Is she getting ready to go out? (Time to start pacing.) She's finishing dinner now—maybe there's something left for me. (I'll just go sit subtly on her feet.) It impresses me, too, that my dogs can tell perfect time within fifteen minutes of dinner, walk time and my bedtime. Dogs are smart. (In fact, those I live with these days seem to be able to count the number of times my phone rings: steady, regularly spaced rings are normal, requiring no action; two quick rings are the signal that someone's coming up the elevator and it's time to go berserk; three stuttery rings are the fax machine, which every so often is fun to watch.) And I'm amused by every dog I see trotting purposefully down the street as if it knows exactly where it's going and what excellent thing it's going to do or find or eat when it gets there.

So Millard and I were pretty comfortable with our dogs. In the thirty or so years since I'd consigned Fluffy to one hairy floor, we'd come to believe that we'd experienced, and more or less successfully dealt with, every possible type of dog behavior and problem:

Aggression
Anxiety
Shedding
Humping
House soiling
House destruction
Clothing destruction
Carpet soiling
Dog sick (which, for obvious reasons, I
    haven't dwelled on much)
Dog sickness
Dog loss

Emma had stopped eating.

We called the vet and the vet found a lump.

We started chemo, and after her first injection, Millard sat on the carpet in the living room with Emma cradled in his arms and said—to no one in particular—"We'll spend whatever it takes."

We did. But nothing helped. There was no help for our gentle Emma, who spent her last days crouched in the niche between a table and a chair on the cool tiles of the hall. Norah tried to soothe her poor face with a damp washcloth, but Jimmy Cagney and Juno wouldn't go near her. And when she stopped eating, when the tumors became too numerous, when they were on top of her head and around her eyes, I called the vet who came to the house and took her away.

I can't forgive myself for not going with her.

Millard made it a point to not be at home.

Miscellaneous thinkers and writers have commented on the configuration of the Heaven to which our lost, loved animals go.

Pablo Neruda had this to say about a favorite dog:

> . . . but now he's gone with his shaggy coat,
> his bad manners and his cold nose,
> and I, the materialist, who never believed
> in any promised heaven in the sky
> for any human being,
> I believe in a heaven I'll never enter.
> Yes, I believe in a heaven for all dogdom
> where my dog waits for my arrival
> waving his fan-like tail in friendship.

And from the Koran:

> There is no beast on earth nor bird which
> flieth with its wings, but the same is a
> people like unto you, and to the Lord
> shall they return.

My favorite is from Martin Luther:

> Be thou comforted, little dog. Thou too, in
> resurrection, shall have a little golden tail.

Somewhere, Emma wags her golden tail.

But she's buried in our garden, just at that corner of the house where she used to break for glory.

Oh, my Millard was desperate for another Emma. Right away. He hadn't the heart for mourning or the patience to wait. He wouldn't even consider a breed other than a Norfolk, either—one that was easy to housebreak, say? He wanted his Emma back. And I did, too, but I also felt obliged to remind him ever so gently of what had happened post-Cosi.

I said, "You never get the same dog again."

I said, "Mill, every dog is a different little being, just like us."

I reached for Heraclitus: "You never step in the same river twice." Which really wasn't applicable but sounded as if it might be.

I fell back in despair on poor old Thomas Wolfe's "You Can't Go Home Again." (Ditto)

And then, having run out of inappropriate bromides, I reluctantly picked up the phone to call the celebrity Norfolk breeder. And this time, the litter was in Milwaukee and Millard—who wasn't a hugger or a kisser or even a dependable hand-holder—leaped on the first plane to bring back to hug and kiss and cradle in his arms the most beautiful puppy I'd ever seen. She was caramel-coated with exceptionally wide spaced brown eyes, soft droopy ears, and a squeaky, bossy bark. He was so besotted with his treasure that he'd barely let me hold her, and at dinner, the night he brought her home, he elatedly reported that while he was waiting in the Milwaukee airport for his return flight, he'd discovered that a man with a puppy was a chick magnet. He didn't put it that way of course, because that particular locution didn't become widespread till after he died. Nevertheless, he managed to make it a little too clear that he'd have been delighted to sit in airports with his Diva forever.

And we couldn't wait to show off the new baby, so we invited Carolan and Peter, dear old friends (cat people, but still, dear friends) to meet her.

Carolan and Peter arrived in a flurry of coats and scarves, and since we were going out to eat, they waited in the hall while Millard went to get our pup. Diva was so tiny that when he came out of the kitchen holding her lovingly in tenderly cupped hands pressed against his chest, only a paw and a tail peeped out. When he was close enough to Peter to pass her to him without having to risk holding her over the hall's tile floor, he made the hesitant, careful exchange. And Peter, pleased and awkward, gently stroked her little head and body and made the sounds we all make when holding something small and helpless. He held her that way for a minute or so, crooning a little.

Then he dropped her.

Millard stood open-mouthed, his face drained of color. And he got to Diva, lying so still on the floor, half a second before I did.

Peter looked from one to the other of us, bewildered.

"What's the matter?" he said. "Did I do something wrong?"

Carolan, horrified, stared at the ceiling, the walls, her hands.

"Kittens," he looked around defensively, "land on their feet."

Puppies don't.

Diva was struggling to get up, wobbling, staggering and shaking her head so hard her tiny ears were making snapping sounds.

Collapsed on a nearby step, Millard and I sat together, shaking. Shaking our heads as well.

"No, no, Peter. It looks like she's all right. Everything's all right. It was a mistake. Just a mistake."

And she *was* all right. And down the road, I don't think her sky-dive affected Diva's brain in any significant way—unless that's the reason she grew up loving to chase airplanes.

And Carolan and Peter are still my dearest friends.

I don't let them near my dogs.

This newest fur family, like our others, just sort-of got along. Jimmy Cagney and Diva cold-shouldered Juno altogether and lorded it over her because she was just a mongrel, after all, and they were *terriers*—by far the better breed. They did seem to like each other the tiniest bit, however, and although I've just been rattling on about how knowledgeable we'd become about dogs, I could still be surprised. For example, even though Diva and Jimmy Cagney had both been neutered, I walked into the kitchen one day to find them mating—in a "tie," I think it's called. Now I didn't know that de-sexed dogs could do that. Or would want to do that. Though on second thought, I could see that at their separate ends of the tie, they were looking fairly baffled about this arrangement themselves, rather as if—like humans—they were wondering how to get out of this extremely awkward situation as painlessly as possible and would it mean that now they'd have to worry about their relationship.

The magnificent little Diva was pure and simple born alpha dog. Pass by her bowl when she was having her dinner—just glance her way while she was eating, in fact—and you'd be face-to-face with her ancestry, slavering jaws and all. Jimmy Cagney shared those vulpine genes and jaws, but his weren't restricted to quiescent food. There was the time, for example, that Norah saw him take down a little bird in the dog yard.

It was spring again, and as a fledgling swooped by, a sad foot or so too low, Jimmy leaped straight up and crushed it in his jaws. When five or six small birds alighted to gather around its poor remains, Norah came to get me to look and swore it was awake. They were holding a wake. And from that moment on, she referred to Jimmy as "that little rat." (Which, given his name, was appropriate.) Jimmy Cagney sometimes stripped his teeth at Norah, too. And snarled. Though no one did that with Norah and got away with it. She was as tough as he was. Or tougher. She could make her two-year-old granddaughter sit through Mass.

Unaccountably, Millard and I had reached our sixties and, as promised — or at least implied — life had turned golden. I don't think I'd term it the sunset of our lives, exactly. It was more that buttery time between five and seven in the evening when you've put on the Chopin and drifted out the back door for a last whiff of the lilacs. We'd become profoundly comfortable in our at-long-last beautiful house, plus, we had two thriving careers, and Barden had married a girl we loved and was living a worthy, if eccentric, life in the East Village. You know, Millard and I had been sure we'd raised a yuppie (I know those suits are still fresh in your mind) and instead, we got an activist/community-involved/gardening/art appraiser. We must have done something right.

No children yet, but I hoped. And hoped.

As to our canine children, Millard and Jimmy Cagney and Juno and Diva and I were enjoying any number of three-dog nights. And to our surprise and delight, our garden had matured. Or should I say the few things that had survived those first ten years had matured because, having killed off scores of tender, unsuspecting perennials and shrubs, we'd found ourselves unexpectedly successful with roses. Climbers had become our specialty, and we were proud to count more than fifty varieties growing over the house, the porches, the garage, the boathouse, the dog run, and if it had only stood still long enough, the car. Come June, when we threw an annual fireworks bash, their scent was old rose and ambrosia.

Millard and I shared jointly in their care: I chose and bought them (naturally); I planted them, fed them, sprayed them (sorry), picked them and arranged them. He got the hard part: the painful and painstaking job of tying them in and pruning the canes. One Father's Day, I presented him with the horticultural equivalent of a bulletproof vest—elbow-length leather rose-pruning gloves. But macho guy that he liked to think he was, he never put them on. Which is why, after a long day on the ladder in the sun, his green tool belt slung low on his oldest jeans and trailing stray ends of rose ties and kelly green string, he'd come banging through the screen door for a beer—happy, sunburned, sweaty and covered in war wounds— having once again done battle with Nature and emerged if not victorious elated.

❀   ❀   ❀

Early in the summer of 2000, as I eased the car up the drive on my way to run an errand, I happened to glance across the lawn and saw Millard on his ladder. In the curve of his back as he leaned to catch a wayward stem, I glimpsed, with a stab of pain, incipient frailty.

Was he smaller?

Was his lovely soft, black hair glinting with gray in the sunshine?

Or is this hindsight?

I was getting older, too, after all. And along with its taking longer and longer each day to look the same, I was increasingly breakable. In fact, one afternoon about two weeks later, I reached to snip a choice pink rose at the top of a long flight of porch stairs, and because the tread I was standing on was narrower than the others (who knew?), I lost my footing and slid-tumbled-fell to the bottom.

Broken ankle, for sure.

And where was Millard?

Just around the corner. Though of course he wouldn't hear me call. Scrabbling painfully across the driveway and onto the lawn, I finally, with much waving and yelling, caught his eye. But after trying to pick me up a few times — I'm not exactly featherlight — Millard scratched his head, wiped his palms on his jeans, and ever the engineer, went to find the wheelbarrow. We maneuvered me into it and feeling stupid and hurting like hell (me), laughing at the dumbness of it all (us) and cursing that stair tread (him), we trundled to the car and went to get it set.

I wouldn't mention this incident except that it put me on crutches for the rest of that summer, and I may have been so focused on getting myself up and down our various staircases and in and out of cars to sit in the bleakly furnished waiting rooms of therapists and orthopods that I wasn't paying sufficient attention when Millard began to complain that the comfortable new easy chair I'd bought him for his birthday was, unaccountably, giving him a backache.

Still, I did snap to attention on that balmy night in late July when, during our usual companionable dinner on the porch, he pushed himself back from his half-full plate and, smiling at me, remarked:

"You know, I'm still hungry. I *feel* like eating more, but I'm full."

He tapped his stomach lightly and turned to watch a blue heron alight on the bulkhead.

❖   ❖   ❖

We were having a favorite dinnertime standby that night: my mother's pasta with meat sauce, a dish that Millard loved. You've met it once before, back in the sixties, when we still called it spaghetti. But no, I'm not about to stop to give you the recipe here and wouldn't, even if this were that sort of book. Because something dire had flashed through my mind: some old, barely remembered warning about being hungry but feeling full. The next day, pricked by unease, I made Millard an appointment with a gastroenterologist.

Who called me the following evening wanting to be solicitous but having no talent whatsoever for such niceties.

"I'm calling about the images we got from Millard's MRI. The radiologist thinks he sees a lesion on his pancreas."

My brain stopped. In the skies above, galaxies stood still.

"What does that mean—a lesion?"

"It means there's a mass of some sort."

I fell to my knees.

"Do you want to tell him or should I?"

"I'll tell him."

"I'm sorry."

"Yes."

❈   ❈   ❈

And then, not giving myself a chance to breathe or think or find some presence of mind, I reached for the phone and called Barden. "Hold on," he told me. "I'll drive right out."

And after that I sat. And sat. And waited for the sound of Millard's car on the drive. And for a good five minutes after he banged through the back door, I listened to him rattling on about his day and the weather and the mail. From somewhere underwater, I heard him pocketing his keys and opening the fridge and I let him have long minutes as I watched old films unwind in my head; old films where secondary characters conspire not to tell the hero how very sick he is and he never knows.

When had that changed? Not everyone has to know. Or wants to.

And then, with all my heart, I yearned to be in some old movie. I yearned to have been born mute. I yearned for him to riffle through the mail forever.

"Dr. Wells called," I said. "He said that something turned up on the MRI."

He turned, interested.

"It's a mass."

He blinked.

"He thinks it's pancreatic cancer."

He asked.
"Maybe a year."

This wasn't real. We stood on our beautiful porch and smiled and squinted at each other in the hot late light off the water. Then we sat on the glider and slowly rocked and acted out a scene I didn't know we knew.

"Is there anything you'd like to do?" I asked. "Anywhere you'd like to go?"

"Nowhere at all."

"I thought a fishing trip, maybe . . ."

"Nowhere. Really."

"What can I do for you, dear?"

"Nothing, I guess."

And he smiled at me.

Millard smiled through Barden's hugs and tears. And two days later, he smiled as we drove to the cancer hospital to meet the oncologist, although I think he smiled mainly because I needed a wheelchair (goddamned ankle) and he had to push me in it through the hospital.

"I'll bet everyone who sees us thinks you're the sick one." He laughed. "How can I be so sick and not feel sick at all?"

We didn't know. He went to work and played tennis and pruned the roses and continued to smile all through the six weeks we waited for the "top pancreatic cancer surgeon" in New York to return from his vacation and operate. (I wonder how it happens that everyone always gets the "top" man? Who gets all those second-best men? Or god forbid, the third?)

Millard even managed to smile after the surgery when, a mere forty minutes into what was to have been his three-hour operation, he woke up in the recovery room, looked at the clock and realized they had simply closed him up and sent him home to die.

"We never thought of this one, did we?" he asked me, smiling.

After that, there were the visits to the specialists and nutritionists, and the highly recommended "grief therapist," whose advice for us was: "It's all right to feel sad."

Sad? *Sad??!!*

Ripped to flaming shreds, rather.

Unspeakable, rather.

Intolerable.

"This will happen to you someday," I wanted

to say, right before I wanted to slap her fatuous face. "Talk to me then about 'sad.'"

And as Millard went faithfully to work—how he loved that busy, noisy plant—I, in my spare time—and I was somehow awash in spare time— was hungrily on the Web, tracking down the pitiably few survivor Web sites; poring through densely unreadable medical publications in search of heartening or possibly useful news; forcing myself to read badly written articles about bizarre holistic cures in fifth-world countries. And all those free-floating new drugs in the pipeline, all those miraculous chemo mixtures, all those extracts of iguana tail, those toes of frog and blind worm's sting; not to mention the harrowing surgeries that, if you were a candidate for them, sometimes worked and sometimes killed; all those life stories and wrenching, far-more-common death stories. And Millard came home from work every night feeling, looking and seeming healthy. Sick? He hadn't lost a pound. He had no symptoms save that barely-worth-mentioning unease in his easy chair and an inability to eat as much as he liked. Weeks turned into a couple of months while we tried convincing ourselves that this was indeed happening.

He was well.

"How can I feel so fine and be so sick?" he

asked over and over, smiling, as we continued to do the usual things.

One Friday night, we went to see *Space Cowboys.*

I thought he'd love it: a quartet of senior astronauts with Clint Eastwood. Rockets, old guys, outer space. What could be bad? Three-quarters of the way through the picture, one of the heroes decides to sacrifice his life for his fellow astronauts because, unknown to his friends, he has pancreatic cancer and won't be alive much longer anyway. Stricken in the flickering dark, I looked sideways to see Millard grinning at me.

"How'd you find this one? Thanks a lot!"

Right after they'd closed him up and sent him home, I'd started serious lobbying to get him into a Phase I trial for a new pancreatic cancer drug that was then being studied by a well-known researcher at a major Manhattan medical center. New drugs require a three-stage protocol on their road to earning (or not) FDA approval. In Phase I of such testing, patients are given increasing doses of the new drug to determine if it's safe and what the maximum tolerable dosage is. She was just beginning Phase I of a new protocol, and I was desperate to get us in. It was the proverbial grasping at straws, but there was the merest possibility that this *could* be The Drug. If that were the case, he might have months or years. Or life, perhaps. So on the October day when we met with god herself and learned we'd been accepted into the protocol, we were over the moon with hope. After leaving the hospital, we floated giddily into a dark bar across the street where we toasted our luck, our resolve to fight and unspoken, our love. How I longed then, not to own, not to care for, but to *be* Lassie: to crawl across this thinning ice and pull Millard by his sleeve to safety, with my fists or with my teeth or with my love.

When I was seventeen and Millard twenty-one, we'd spent sweet summer evenings sitting in dark bars in Pittsburgh with "Jamaica Farewell" and "Day-O" floating on the smoke-and-promise air. We always sat together at the bar, drinking, sampling our maturity; drinking, falling artlessly in love.

As a token of his love, Millard had created a very realistic looking fake Georgia driver's license for me with which I could indulge in Brandy Alexanders while he knocked back the tougher stuff, Dewars on the rocks. My god, I was impressed. His white linen jacket, his button-down blue shirt and madras tie, the brush of his dark crew cut and the warmth of his soft drawl; his tan, his pipe, his dimple: He made me faint with airy hope. Millard and the Brandy Alexanders.

Now we rarely drank and seldom sat in bars.

But that night, for the first time in a thousand years, we sat knee to knee. Beneath our entwined hands, the bar top reflected us dimly.

And we cried.

Denial is the first stage.

He didn't last long enough for us to encounter the second, for almost immediately after his first dose of the miracle drug, he wound up in the emergency room, where his blood work revealed he'd had a dangerous reaction to the poison. It was, after all, poison.

And Barden and I were terrified to see him so sick. He'd never been sick. Never had flu. Never broken a bone. Never had a headache. And our new best friend, the famous researcher, seemed to have been frightened, too, because when next we went to the hospital for his treatment, there were different meds in the chemo drip.

"But we were in Dr. X's protocol," I said to the nurse.

"Oh no," she replied, all officiousness and innocence, "I don't know anything about that. This is what's down on his chart, and this is all I can give him."

The following day I learned we'd been dropped from the trial like the infamous hot potato, and our researcher—our savior—hadn't even bothered to let us know.

I understand the woman.

I do.

You don't want to be killing test subjects with your trial drugs.

But it seemed to us that we'd been expelled from the potential of Paradise without an explanation. Even Adam and Eve got an explanation.

And Millard slipped beneath the ice.

Immediately after that single Phase I chemo treatment, he was suddenly, truly sick. And daily grew sicker.

We had to leave a party halfway through dinner.

At work, they told me, he was dozing through the day.

He was noticeably jaundiced, increasingly paler and weaker.

He spent a disquieting amount of time lying mutely on a sofa in the sunroom, looking out the window.

The great metropolitan hospital where he was being treated for what, till now, had been an invisible disease, had built a falsely soothing waterfall in its marble lobby and had hidden speakers piping in whiny New Age music. It had unfailingly pleasant and interested people behind every desk. It had empathetic nurses (mostly) and smiling attendants. Despite this scripted goodwill, the next time I took Millard to the third floor for his eight A.M. exam, everyone—every one of those thoroughly coached, well-meaning people—dropped the ball.

The sweet administrators at the desk misplaced his paperwork. The busy doctor hadn't written the scrip and had gone out for lunch. And long after lunch, the so-sorry nurse had forgotten to send someone to pick up the prescription from the hospital pharmacy, and when she did at last, the scrip wasn't ready. And no one realized, somehow, that we were waiting . . . and waiting. Maybe it was none of these or all of these—but there we were, still waiting in that deceptively cozy, crappy waiting room at six thirty that same evening—Millard lying uncomfortably on a narrow banquette, dozing, and me, for possibly the first time in my life, wanting truly . . . truly . . . to kill. We'd fallen through the cracks of the oh-so-perfect hospital.

I bent down and spoke softly in Millard's ear.

"I'm going to find someone."

"What? What? Wait. I'll go with you."

He squinted into the light, trying to shake off his stupor. Then, with real effort, he stood and walked with me back through the labyrinth of hallways and small rooms where scores of patients still waited to see the great doctor and then, farther on, into the long corridor that led to the central office.

I approached one of the kinder patient liaison people and took her aside. She seemed, now, to be the only one there.

I smiled politely.

"You know, we've been waiting out there the whole day for my husband's meds. Do you, or does anyone else here, know what's happening?"

"Oh, I'm so sorry. I'll see what I can find out for you." And she turned to pick up the phone.

I looked around at the tidy, empty office; at the neat desks and the cheerful curtains and the dead computer screens.

And all of a sudden, I was yelling.

"What do you *mean* doing this to us?! Don't you know how hard this is for us even without sitting through hours and hours of these screwups?! Don't you see how tired he is? That he ought to be at home having dinner? That he ought to be in bed? Not lying on a bench at six thirty at night waiting for these stupid pills?"

The nice woman was actually cowering a little, and out of the corner of my eye, I caught Millard's shocked, pale face.

Oh, his face was lovely! There was discomfort and embarrassment there, but there was also shy joy. In our whole life together, he had never seen me yell at stranger.

"I'm so, so sorry," said the woman, almost in tears. "Oh, you're right. I'm really so sorry. I'll see what I can do to get you out of here. This is terrible. You're right. It's terrible."

I was right.

I was right?

My god, I wanted to yell some more. I needed to yell some more. But I wasn't used to the thrill of confrontation, and in the next minute, I'd dissolved into a teary, apologetic splutter.

We finally did get our meds, and later that night, as I numbly drove my exhausted husband home — his head thrown back on the seat, his eyes closed — I brooded on the hospital's lapse. Could it be that casual inhumanity is standard at all over-taxed urban treatment centers, or is it inadvertently but subtly reserved for those who've been sent home to die?

When I'd first begun to investigate medical care for Millard, a physician acquaintance had offered me the most unwelcome, hateful advice: Don't worry about getting the "best" or most highly recommended doctor, he said. Just look for that person who'll be there for your midnight phone call; the guy who'll show up when things get hard and you need him to be there.

I'd fumed after that call. *Not* what I'd wanted to hear. I'd been hoping to be told about the godly physician who could save us. And here was this friend-of-a-friend telling me there was nothing I could do beyond hoping for a hand to hold.

I understood him perfectly now though.

And it wasn't too late.

That's why we walked out of the great and famous hospital with its Stepford attendants and its waterfall and its commitment to research over humanity and found a physician who seemed truly compassionate; a doctor who cared for Millard but didn't promise anything and didn't smile any more than seemed necessary to pleasant professional conversation; a doctor who told us earnestly and honestly, "We'll get you through this."

I've thought about those subtle words many times.

Millard was constantly drowsy now; asleep more than he was awake. And this meant, rather strangely and perhaps for the first and only time in our life together, that he didn't get Socratic about everything I did. It was almost a relief, I admit it. Nevertheless, once, as I was driving him to the city for yet one more doctor's appointment, he awoke from his stupor, lifted his head, looked around, and asked, "Why aren't you passing that truck?"

Why, indeed.

Although ask him a direct question now and he could barely rouse himself to say, "I'll do whatever my wife wants." He'd always done that, you know. But never actually said so.

On an ordinary Thursday in November, as the country geared up for the Bush election, Millard drove to work and around noon, he called me from his desk.

"Could you come and get me? I need to come home."

As I helped him into the car, he smiled apologetically and leaned his head back on the headrest, smiling still, and slept. Once we were home, he stretched out on the living room sofa and slipped into a doze. An hour or so later, I was walking past him with a glass of water in my hand when he opened his eyes, smiled and asked:

"Where are you going with that"— he searched for the word—"book?"

I slammed the glass down so hard the water sloshed over the tabletop, then I ran to the phone and called the new doctor who, with chilling urgency in his voice said, "I think he may have developed hepatic encephalopathy. Bring him in to the emergency room right away. I'll arrange for his admission."

And so, for a final time, we made that familiar drive to the city and Millard was admitted as immediately as they ever do such things. But there seemed to be no beds in the hospital that day, even for the very, very sick. So some very, very efficient nurses put my barely conscious Millard on a gurney and wheeled him into the ER, where, I was told, we'd just have to wait. Sobbing audibly, I trailed the gurney toward a curtained cubicle as a Latina woman waiting with her family called after me, "Don't cry, Mami, everything will be all right."

"Mami?" Was I a Mami? I wept.

The impressive nurse in charge didn't want me crying either.

"If you insist on crying, you can't stay in the ER. You'll have to wait outside."

Now *there* was a powerful weapon; one she'd very likely wielded effectively a thousand times before. It impressed me enough that I choked on my tears for nine long hours, during which Millard drifted into unconsciousness and we waited and waited and waited for a bed.

Maddeningly, there was nowhere in that big emergency room for family to sit. There was the busy central desk, the tiny roomlets, each encapsulating its discrete and frightening misery, a great deal of menacing electrical equipment and within a fairly large space, nothing to sit on but a few rolling stools. I discovered the hard way (Ms. Large and Bossy again) that these were off-limits to everyone but staff. For legal reasons. Though wouldn't you love to know how an adult could manage to injure herself on a rolling stool? Push off hard, maybe, and shoot across the room straight into a wall? Roll into a syringe-wielding nurse? Fall a terrifying eighteen inches to the floor? But there they all sat—empty. While I didn't. Then, at around two thirty A.M., drained, weary, and stiff from leaning against walls and tables, I eased myself down to the floor at the foot of Millard's gurney. And it took about five seconds for the No-Crying Nurse to sniff me out.

"You can't sit on the floor," she raged. "There might be blood on the floor!!! Fatal diseases!!

I looked around. There *was* blood on the floor, in fact. Suspicious-looking shades-of-yellow things, as well.

She was a good deal bigger than me and hadn't liked me from the get-go. She was fighting mad, Miss Nurse. But I, grandly, was madder.

"Goddammit, I'm going to sit here if I want to, and you know what? I don't give a shit if I get a disease!"

"Get up!" she hollered, looming over me, face in my face, hands on huge hips. "Get up, or I'm going to call Security!"

There wasn't much staff in the emergency room at that hour. At the word "security," those few that were in the area looked up from their monitors and murmured conversations and leaned ever so slightly in our direction.

I was filled with something like righteous testosterone, like nuclear fury, and I was getting ready to stand up and . . . push her, maybe? . . . hit her? . . . when Millard, who hadn't spoken since he'd called a glass a book, sat straight up on his narrow gurney, and peering over its foot to find me sitting on the floor at his feet, turned to the giantess, smiled and said in a louder than normal voice, and emphatically:

"Let my wife sit wherever she wants."
He was cogent as hell.
He was Zeus.

He lay back down and left me once more.

But she looked at him in shocked surprise, turned her back on us both and walked away. And I continued to sit there, and after another hour or so, we got a bed.

We only stayed in the hospital for a couple of days. Long enough for friends to gather on the chairs at the foot of Millard's bed and long enough for him to have one of those unexpected returns to clarity in which he sat up, looked around and observed: "Looks like you're all sitting shivah." Then falling back on his pillows, he slept again, leaving me laughing and everyone else faintly embarrassed.

Long enough for Barden to bring his dad homemade marijuana brownies (the handy neighborhood dope peddler being an advantage of a downtown 'hood). He didn't tell his father they were good for him or tell him what was in them, so when Millard took a bite, spit it on the sheet and pronounced it awful, I took the brownies home, stuffed them in the back of the freezer and months later, looking for a little pain relief for myself, learned that Norah had eaten them all.

Long enough for one of the staff doctors to gather his class around my husband's bedside to watch and take notes while he asked an awake and smiling and wishing-to-be-helpful Millard to hold his uncontrollably flapping hands out in front of him for them to see. This humiliating little trick was one they could use, he told them, to diagnose liver involvement when they all grew up to be wonderfully callous MDs themselves.

Long enough for me to know that nothing else could be done.

When the palliative care team came to see me, all soft voices and practiced solicitude, I ordered an ambulance and took him home. I didn't want him in a hospital anymore, this hospital or any hospital. And despite the fact that by then Millard had fallen into a persistent stupor, he still seemed to be able to hear, and he still occasionally opened his eyes. And when he did, his mind was, surprisingly, very much his own: clear, unaware of and untroubled by his condition. He had no idea he was dying.

And he was so sweetly overjoyed to be back in our own bedroom. He smiled broadly, visibly thrilled to be at home and in our bed.

That evening, when Norah tiptoed in with an unusually quiet Diva under her arm and we set her down beside him and she licked his fingers, I could see how he loved it. I sat next to them both on the edge of the bed and fed him some spoonfuls of vanilla ice cream. Just a few; he wasn't hungry. But he smiled. I gave him small doses of morphine. I fed him ice chips. And I sang to him. Folk songs. Old songs. One old song that made him sad, I think, because he asked me not to sing it.

I told him I was there with him. I begged him to stay. And then he drifted off to a deepening sleep as I lay next to him, awake all night and listening for his slow, slowing, slower breaths.

In the bright morning . . . smiling . . . he was gone.

Turning my face away, I rose from my lifelong place beside him on our bed and walked away. I wouldn't look. But I did look at Juno, Jimmy and Diva, lying stretched on the carpeted bedroom floor, untroubled and unconcerned. How could they be alive when Millard wasn't? Why were they alive? Those . . . dogs.

Why was I?

Chapter Nine

Dog Person

Afterward, I was glad Millard died before I did. I wouldn't have wanted him to go through that grief.

In those first agonies, Norah looked after me and protected me from the unbearable things, and Barden did, too. From the painful phone calls to old friends and business associates, for instance. From the ordering and distributing of the hateful death certificates; from the wretched emptyings of closets and drawers. I stopped being able to work, and instead, autodidact to the end, drove out daily to buy books on widowhood: advice, memoirs, self-help, all of it. Nothing worked. Of course.

For a few minutes back there in the beginning,

I remember yearning to believe in a Heaven and regretting that I couldn't.

For a while, I thought about joining Millard in the small local cemetery where I'd left him; for a while, I joined a grief group, instead.

Once, I tried traveling. Lonely beauties. Lonely meals. Lonely beds. Lonely.

And nothing helped.

I didn't stop looking though; even years later.

I had great hopes for Joan Didion, for example. But she let me down: she wrote Death, obliquely, to death. And everything else I read let me down, as well. Because none of the books or essays or blogs, eventually, had the answers I was looking for. Of course I didn't know the questions—and don't, to this day—so that may not surprise you. Though I think they may be on the order of: How do you get through each day? And night? And when will this be over? And why do I have to live this leftover life?

So what I can tell you about grief is this:

It brings regret and guilt for all the widows you never wrote to because you didn't know.

It is anguish beyond your imaginings.

It lasts as long you live.

❄   ❄   ❄

And as lacerating as Millard's loss was and remains, it's left me, puzzlingly, with only a few discernable scars:

I now sleep with the television on all night, my set permanently tuned to old movies, so when I waken at three A.M. and open my eyes and begin to think — I can't. I can only slip into *Marie Antoinette* or *Some Like It Hot* or *G.I. Joe.*

And I can't bear to look at gardens. And roses. Especially in spring.

And instead of playing sports or going to movies or reading and sipping tea, I write all weekend long.

I still wear my wedding ring.

Aside from those few quirks, I discovered in the intervening years that, much as I might have preferred not to, I managed.

Except for Jimmy Cagney.

That little dog was becoming more and more like his namesake. Not your George M. Cohan in *Yankee Doodle Dandy,* but the psychopath from *White Heat.* My Jimmy had begun to bite not just dogs but people, which was very bad and very scary and worse, possibly actionable. And which

I accepted as my own fault for coddling the cutest puppy that ever was and letting him think I was Cody Jarrett's ma. He'd bitten a friend and another friend's baby, neither badly, but I wasn't about to wait for badly.

For at long last, it had become clear to me that all those Cassandras were right; the Jack Russell wasn't the breed for me, no "probably" about it. And the problem was never really with the dogs. As the naysayers had more than hinted, the problem was with me: for expecting too much; for loving a breed and a physical type and a personality rather than knowing myself.

How could I have actually thought I was feisty like my Jacks, when in truth, I was mild, citified, cowardly and at times, possibly, even, sweet? I'd hoped—assumed—my dogs would be like me, and I'm told that there are many more Jacks that are these days (well, maybe not so cowardly). But the Jacks I've owned, at least, ought to have come with a warning: For Advanced Owners Only. Or For Households That Include Deep-Voiced, Leather-Gloved Men. Or maybe just For Households with Men.

I missed mine.

With aching regret but a budding hope of imminent relief, I phoned Jack Russell Rescue. (In the fourteen years since we'd loved Cosi, some fine

and noble soul had created Jack Russell Rescue—
which reinforced my suspicion that I wasn't the
only owner who'd turned out to be "wrong for the
breed.") But even JRR wouldn't take a biter.

Friends—mostly cat friends—suggested I put
him down, the awful answer for aggressive dogs.

But wait a minute. He wasn't tearing anyone's
throat out. He wasn't rabid. He was still the most
adorable Jack in the world.

And just as I was getting a little panicky and
had stopped speaking to my cat friends, I learned
about a Long Island newspaper that didn't charge
an advertising fee to people giving dogs away. So
I tried an ad in the Pets section:

*Male Jack Russell terrier for adoption; cute, neu-
tered and small; wants a home with no children and
needs to be an only dog"* (Oh all right. He'd been
attacking Diva and Juno, too.)

In case you need further proof that the aver-
age person doesn't read, I got six calls from people
with kids, plus one woman who wanted to know
what a Jack Russell was, and was it a dog? She
asked this in spite of the fact that she'd obviously
gotten my number from the "Dog" section of Pets.

And then, magically, I got a call from a young
woman: a schoolteacher. Her father had just lost
his mean little Yorkie and was looking for a substitute. Could she come to see my Jimmy?

When can you come? Today?! Come today!

And when she showed up at the door, young, sweet and good-natured, but canny, too—she was a teacher, after all—I asked her to wait in the living room while I went to get The Little Rat, who was confined to the kitchen because, when the doorbell rang, he might have attacked her, or me, or Juno, or less threateningly but more messily, merely piddled on her leg. Leaving none of this to chance, I tucked his square little body securely under my arm, carried him out to where she was sitting on the sofa and set him gently on the floor at her feet.

His white bottom wriggled in sheer delight.

"What an adorable little boy," said the unsuspecting schoolteacher, leaning toward him to scratch his ears.

I held my breath.

With which, Jimmy Cagney rolled over on his back and peed straight up in the air.

Oh god, I thought, running to the kitchen.

Where are the damn paper towels?

But can you believe it! She wanted him! She loved him! She—WOW!

And as I tore through the house, gathering up his toys, his bed, his leash and bowl (maybe she wanted my own bed and toys, too?), I could scarcely believe my luck. She was taking him. To her father. To Queens. To far away.

And the moment her car pulled out of the driveway, I called Barden.

"Are you sitting down? Someone just adopted Jimmy Cagney!"

After a measured silence, Barden replied, "Listen, Mom. Leave the house right now, go out for dinner and then to a movie and don't come home until it's really, really late."

And I took his advice. You'd better believe I took his advice. Though for the next two or three weeks (well, for most of the following year) my heart stopped any time the caller ID showed the Queens exchange. But she kept him. And it tickles me now to think of her father — in my imagination, one of those gray-haired, mustachioed men in a woolen cap and maybe with a cane, an American version of the *Country Life* gents — taking the air in Queens with a bandy-legged velociraptor named Jimmy Cagney.

So here's a confession: About a year and a half after Millard died, I tried to adopt myself out as well.

I went online.

What attracted me to the online dating services was that they offered an absolutely expenditure-free shopping opportunity while simultaneously exercising my novelty-seeking gene. Naïve as I was, I actually expected salvation to come from one of those new online dating services: something on the order, say, of a six-foot-four, handsome, witty, smart, younger (?) man of sufficient means, who'd also—by the way—love me. What I found instead, and I know this isn't news, were endless and flattering pictures of old men in baseball caps (hmm), old men in sailboats, old men in T-shirts in front of the Louvre, old men in shorts at the Taj Mahal, old men with many, many grandchildren, old men with dogs (hmm). And mainly . . . old men. A lot of plump, a lot of comb-overs, a lot of facial hair and they all looked alike. Would I have found any of them attractive back when? And who really cared? Because what I wanted was my marriage back.

Still, among all those ostensibly unmarried men out there, among all those thousands, you'd think there might have been one—only one—as fine as the man I'd lost. Would you believe it, I somehow didn't remember that in the forty-two years Millard and I had been married, I'd never once met another man I liked even half as well as the one I had. Because other men were boring

or unintelligent or not handsome enough or over-
bearing. (Or not argumentative enough?) Which
meant that the odds of my finding a man like Millard at this late date were nil.

I talked on the phone with several contenders, though. We small-talked endlessly about their
incredibly wicked former wives, their ungrateful
children, slobbery mastiffs, why my callers loved
sailing, why I didn't like sailing and I even talked
with one man who, after an hour and a half of
mildly promising conversation, confessed that he
had an STD. I didn't actually know what that was.
Uncool, long-married me.

I even took a few of the shinier prospects out
for a trial spin (not Mr. STD), learning, in the
process, more than I ever wanted to know about
the rules of cricket, the life of a sixties CIA operative, long walks on the beach and fine wines,
and New York's divorce courts. Some of them
were even fairly nice; some took me to dinner at
a diner, and you know I like diners. But I usually eat a grilled cheese sandwich and a Coke,
and when they accepted my offer to pay for myself . . . well, hey. Some, for one long-married
"virgin," were a little too anxious to get physical (I missed that seventies moment), and one
wanted a producer for his play. The one I should
never have gone out with at all was the one who

told me that in his youth, he'd been madly in love with Gina Lollobrigida in *Trapeze*. (See author photo.) None of them cared to know much about me, and at the end of the day and the evening, I contented myself with the truism that after a certain age, a woman has a choice: be either a nurse or a purse. Though honestly, I would have been thrilled to be either or both for a Millard. But they weren't making them like that anymore. What a rare breed he seemed to have been. A breed that was, sadly, extinct.

You're out there shaking your finger at me, aren't you? Reminding me of what I've been telling you for the last two hundred pages about replacing a love you've lost.

Casting around for love's smaller crumbs, and more out of loneliness than smarts, I decided finally to go ahead and adopt that greyhound I'd always wanted.

Hell with the road.

I'd be super-watchful.

And besides, in researching the breed, I'd discovered that some of the males are almost as big as a man.

❀   ❀   ❀

In truth, I'd been edging up on my greyhound even before Millard died.

That last year, we'd made some money in the stock market and had impulsively decided to spend some of it on a pair of life-size lead statues of greyhounds. They were tremendously heavy, hundreds of pounds, and they'd go outdoors, of course. But they were far from the sort of decorative objects you carry around while trying to decide where to put them because they were so heavy, it took three of us just to move them: Millard, me and Alan, the saintly, patient dog trainer who'd been trying to help me turn Jimmy Cagney into a domestic pet. Alan was good with all the dogs, in fact, and had been working with Juno and Diva on the "sit" and "come." Jimmy, you might have guessed, did neither.

I'd picked two good potential spots for our sculptures, the first of which was wrong, naturally. So after about an hour of struggling and being insanely careful not to bump either of their long, thin, very much in-the-way tails, we managed to maneuver the two statues into what looked like a brilliant position just near the entrance to the house. And in fact, they looked beautiful there. Composed of softish, dove-gray lead and backed, now, by gray house paint and green-black ivy, they were (almost) as beautiful as the McCoy.

That's when Alan stepped back and considered the dogs and their placement.

He looked at us. We looked at him.

We looked at them. We nodded.

"Stay," he said.

So they did.

My new and soulful real dog, whom I found being fostered by a Connecticut greyhound adoption group, was a loser. Racing greyhound puppies (whose ears are tattooed with their birthdates and litter numbers) are customarily grown-on for a year, trained for a year, and raced for a year. After that, if they're not winners or if they've broken a leg or hate to run, they're euthanized.

They are.

But greyhounds make divine house pets. They simply want to lie around on lots of pillows. I've heard, too, that many are good with cats and hamsters and even birds. Nevertheless, because their early training reinforces their prey drive—i.e., they've learned to chase small furry things like rabbits, squirrels, cats, and um . . . little dogs—people who own Norfolk terriers are well advised to be circumspect. Which is why, when I drove up to the leafy environs of Hartford to choose my life's second largest companion, I took Diva along for a test. Carolan, my bridesmaid and funniest friend, rode shotgun, for company and for laughs.

Diva hated cars as much as Cosi had loved them and upchucked the whole way there; and when there was nothing left to chuck, she retched. Let me assure you that I never would have subjected her to such misery except for safety's sake. Millard's Diva wasn't going to be anyone's dinner. I'd had my fill of blood and tears.

When we arrived at the modest ranch house where lovingly modest "parents" fostered incoming ex-racers, I was offered a choice of eight handsome, sad dogs, and after peering into several dark crates at gorgeous, scruffy greys, I winnowed it down to a "final three" based on their reputed gentleness, their sex, and—well, you know me—their beauty. Then the finalists were muzzled and leashed and brought out to the front lawn to meet Diva, who—still reeling from her miserable ride—was more than a little subdued. Three long, tall racers, never having met a small dog before—or seen mirrors, windows, water or a loving hand—showed intense interest in Diva. They approached her, heads down, noses working, and as they neared, my frazzled Diva, taxed well beyond her minim of terrier patience, backed off, lifted her tiny head, and reached for her high C. Only one of those dogs—the largest—leaped in the air and tried to hide.

That was my man.

So Ajax (I'm improving, don't you think? His track name was Crabby Jeff) huddled in the far corner of the backseat, away from the crated but threatening Diva and threw up the whole way home. Which was why, from Hartford to Long Island, Carolan and I sang him terrible Tony Bennett songs and poorly harmonized Christmas carols. Which didn't help.

And I thought he might just throw up again when he saw the stairs to my front door. Track dogs, you may not know, have never seen stairs, and it took us fifteen minutes or so to shove him, coax him with biscuits (wholly ineffective as bribes, since he'd never seen biscuits either) and eventually to hoist all eighty, gangly pounds of him into the house.

It took Ajax an extraordinarily long time to get used to living somewhere other than in a crate. On the other hand, if there can be any advantage at all to a greyhound's growing up in a crate and being allowed out only to relieve himself and race, it's that housebreaking is a virtual snap. So Ajax housebroke immediately (such a blessing in a big dog) and was as good with Juno as any other of our dogs had been—which meant that he ignored her. But he adored Diva. He loved putting her entire head in his mouth best of all.

Shall I compare him to a summer's day?

Ajax is tall. My hand at my side finds his head just beneath. He's muscular. Or he was then. He's less so now that he no longer runs. But his coat, with its stripes like a tiger's on tawny fur, is beautiful; nowhere near as dull and dusty as when he first came to me. It's silky and short and healthy and sleek. He's quite long, so he moves like a tiger, too, and has trouble making turns in narrow halls. He's scarred, as all track dogs seem to be, because racers fight, though I hope not over food. He shares Juno's I'm-dying shriek, but he's effortlessly elegant. Except when he sleeps, and his head drapes over the rolled arm of his oversize bed and his long pink tongue hangs sideways out of his mouth. Or when he's cleaning his nether parts and gets his hind leg stuck on his head behind his ears and doesn't know how to get it off.

Ajax talks to me, sometimes, as well. He whimpers and stares with his grave black eyes—but not to tell me how he loves me. Usually just to let me know the door to the john is closed and he needs to get a drink. (Which tells you what a long way I've come since Fluffy.) His eyes are so expressive. I loved the way they widened at his first taste of pizza "bones" or peanut butter. He speaks to me with his eyes and his bruised and tender heart, so I pity his terror of thunderstorms and of other dogs, but I *love* that in all the years we've been together, he's never learned how to put those long front legs up on a counter to eat my dinner while I'm preparing it. (Juno does that.) And he doesn't get up on sofas or chairs either (Juno does that) and is happiest in my bed or by my side. Just like Millard.

Right after I brought Ajax home—within the first two weeks, in fact—the gate to the dog run was left open and he disappeared. Perhaps I haven't mentioned that track greyhounds have never crossed streets or seen cars? So when I discovered him gone, mindless and shaking, I filled my car with treats, grabbed for his leash and drove around our local streets yelling, "Ajax!!! Ajax!!!" Everyone within earshot certainly thought I was selling kitchen cleanser door to door. But sitting on

my heart was fate and death; because this dog—
this gone-missing dog—barely knew my voice, let
alone his own name. And there was that terrible
road. And he was speed itself.

But remember that he'd never seen water? My
next-door neighbors had a pond, and happening
to look out their window, they'd noticed this large,
panicky animal floundering in their pond. Ajax
had tried to run across it.

I took him home, dripping and bewildered,
and double locked the gate.

So it was me and Norah and the dogs now.
And a big house that wasn't all *that* hard to keep.
I'd been well trained, remember. Norah did the
inside, and John and I did the out—and the house
held its own. I gave Norah Millard's huge old station wagon. She was so small she could barely see
over the steering wheel, but it made it so much
easier for her to get to her family and the thrift
shops that she loved. Still, as several seasons came
and did their weathery thing and passed us by, the
house seemed less and less fun to live in. In spring
and summer, the roses grew and bloomed, the
wisteria climbed, the morning glories that Millard
loved seeded themselves and wound carelessly
around windows and porch posts. But I didn't

care to work in the garden alone. I stopped going out on our porch; the gorgeous sunsets across the water made me so melancholy I thought I'd die. Good friends visited and called, and some stayed and some invited me to dinner and to lovely parties and cheered me. For a while.

And it was winter, and Norah and I dug my car out of the snowdrifts on the driveway. And it was fall, and we found a snake in the laundry room and she courageously swept it out while the three of us—Norah, me and the snake—writhed and cringed as I bore it to the driveway in a horribly small dustpan and threw it in the general direction of the grass.

It was another beautiful, beautiful spring and I cried.

And the only marvelous thing was my grandchild.

For here's my second confession.

Between late July, when Millard was diagnosed, and early November, when he died, I hadn't been big on reality, but now and then, I'd let some creep in. Once or twice, I'd even thought ahead.

In 2000, Barden and Catherine had been married for nine remarkably happy years, and they were having so much fun just being together that, very reluctantly and painfully, I'd given up the golden idea of having a grandchild. Of course I couldn't talk to them about it. Mothers and mothers-in-law, you must have heard, need to become really good at smiling a lot and wearing brown.

But with Millard so ill, it came thudding home to me that nothing but a grandchild could continue the thread of his life. Dog-loving genes and novelty-seeking genes were nothing to me now. Millard's genes were the ones that mattered.

It was odd, and I suppose I should have expected it, but when Barden moved out, all those years ago, Millard and he had become close. So close that he'd enjoyed a much more relaxed relationship with our son than I did. They talked together easily on the phone and played tennis and did companionable things with hammers and saws. And, okay, I decided in my jealous heart, that was probably because they hadn't been business partners; because Millard and our son hadn't been in one small office all day for two trying years. Primarily, though, I recognized, in my jealous and wounded heart, it was because Barden would dread me a little forever. Because I was intimidating, I guess. Like my mother.

So Millard had to be the one to ask.

I brought it up. Casually.

"Mill, dear, would you mind telling Barden that you'd really like to have a grandchild?"

"But you know I don't care about having a grandchild."

"I know, dear. But would you think about doing it for me?"

He was silent. Which often, mistakenly or not, I took for assent.

I ought to digress here to explain that throughout the years we were married and even when we were young—though sure, that was the fifties— I called him "dear." I think my mother may have called my father "dear," but he called her "babe," or "hup babe." Hugely outdated.

Does anyone call anyone "dear" today? Cabdrivers, maybe, and other condescending males. I suppose I miss saying it, nevertheless, because I find myself closing phone conversations by calling good friends "dear."

"Good-bye, dear. Talk soon," I say.

So unlike me really.

Anyway, weeks later, I asked Millard if he'd made my devious request of Barden and he told me he had.

Two years after Millard died, I learned that Catherine had had a miscarriage, and my heart broke with theirs. But three years after Millard died, she gave birth to Tucker, whose full name is Tucker Velocity. (One of those inherited gifts, I guess.) In abstruse honor of his dad, Barden tells me, he found the "Velocity" part while leafing through a physics book. And he, alone in the family, calls her "Velo." I call her "sweetheart," "pussycat," "dumpling," "my heart's true joy," and I know that I owe her to Millard.

Yet, once, years later, I asked Barden if, around the time Dad was sick, he'd ever said anything about wanting a grandchild. Barden thought a minute or two. No, he answered.

But don't forget, Barden doesn't remember Tippy.

Juno's face was graying and almost white, Ajax was learning to love having his throat stroked, Diva was enjoying her mature Divahood, and my small human family was ensconced in Alphabet City. I was still writing every day, but what you've heard is true: It's solitary. My life's weather seemed to be turning relentlessly overcast and the outlook was for continuing clouds and showers with too few patches of Tucker. It also seemed to be a very long trip from Avenue D to Long Island.

Although I loved it, of course, when Tucker came, and the dogs loved it, too. When she was small, they were terrified by her crying and would hide when she visited, except for Diva, who would be insanely interested in licking her face—whereupon Tucker would hide. As she got older, though, the only one who found anything about her to object to was Ajax, who minded very much that she made herself comfortable in *his* bed to watch kid movies. When Juno got her lovely breakfast of milk and bread, Tucker would help me prepare it and feed both dogs bits of her own cereal and soothe them and croon to them. A little like me.

Though have I mentioned, she has Millard's olive skin and Millard's perfect fingernails? And she likes to crunch ice.

But between lovely visits, there was that internal weather.

One spring evening, I was talking to my brother, Richard, in St. Louis. He was all fired up at the prospect of maybe selling his house. Maybe he and his wife would live on a houseboat or in a Winnebago, maybe. (That familial gene.) Maybe they'd buy a great town house in the old section of town. Maybe they'd travel the world on bikes. He was so excited and convincing that when we hung up, I began to think about moving myself. Maybe.

Then, with growing certainty and mounting excitement, I turned to Diva, who'd scootched over next to me on the sofa and barked throughout our conversation, and said:

"I think I'll do that, too."

Not the Winnebago part. The selling-the-house part.

And yes, I'd started talking to the dogs.

And no, Richard never moved.

Thus began my Seven Lean Years.

Which I'll spare you because you don't want to know, any more than I did, about the retracted offers, the failures to show up at closings, the suits, the countersuits, the financial losses and the unending accrual of unwelcome, aging angst. But hey, New York City with its doormen and food deliveries is assisted living for single women. But hey, as well, you don't need to hear about the too-large Manhattan apartment I moved to because — hey, I was going to miss my big house (and do you remember what I obviously did not? That I'd once sworn never to live an apartment again?) Then darling Norah, who had moved into the city with me, decided to retire to a condo in Florida to Irish dance with her girlfriends, and even the promise of a lifetime of nightly baked potato dinners wasn't enough to keep her in Manhattan. Neither were the terrific thrift shops. Not even my dogs, and especially Ajax, who needed her desperately to protect him from fire engines and dachshunds, were enough to keep her in New York.

Ajax had become a nervous wreck.

One evening, just as she was taking him out for a walk, one of the doormen dropped a metal tray on the polished marble floor.

"Ajax, in fact, almost broke a leg trying to get away," she told me that night. "I had to hold on with all my strength. Those doormen thought it was so funny! They were laughing at him! So you know what I did? I said, 'You two have shit-all to do here besides make this dog nervous! If you knew the miserable life this poor dog has led . . .' and I walked him out the door."

Norah may not have been from New York City, but she had all the essential attributes for making it there.

Later, she admitted, "I made them some soda bread the next day."

She was from Ireland as well.

Ultimately, though, she was from the East Coast of Florida, where the "whiskey is half price," "all the doctors are drug pushers," and where she can watch all the old movies she loves all day long, and rattle off, under her breath, the names of the grand old stars. Whom she knows better than I do. Which is saying something.

So I was alone.

And I quickly discovered how very too large my new digs were and how really hard it was to handle three dogs on three leashes without losing your dignity and/or falling down.

It was the falling-down part that scared me.

You know those dog walkers with the fifteen dogs? It's always seemed wonderful to me that they manage to handle them all. Then, one day, I looked carefully and saw what I'd never noticed: most of the dogs are pretty much the same size— and *that's* what makes it work. If you're walking a Lab, a retriever and a pointer, it's perfect. If you're walking a greyhound, a Lurcher and a Norfolk, that terrier can walk right underneath the other two. And does. She can wrap her leash around their legs while she's chasing pigeons. And does. And while you're trying to get them all untangled, amid your Juno's shrieks of "don't touch my feet" and your Ajax's loud, deeply peeved barks, one or the other of the big dogs gets around behind you, and like some setup from the Keystone Cops, you just go over. One broken shoulder and five black eyes later, you learn to walk them separately. That's *nine* walks a day.

So that's some of the reason I decided to sell up once more, move to a smaller, cheaper, more central location and simultaneously, move Diva to an airier, less central, very much larger one. Because along with causing me grief on New York's streets, Diva had become so mouthy, so blithely busy peeing on new carpets and—aaarghhh—on my bed, so busy being such a terrier basically, that I needed to find her a country home.

Forgive me, terrier gods. Except for my trio of fighters and biters, there can be no excuse.

And it hasn't escaped my notice that biters in general seem to be less of a problem for other dog lovers than they are for me. Could it just be that it's not that I'm not as much of a Jack Russell person as I thought I was, but that I'm also not as much of an animal person as I want to think I am? Confrontation terrifies me; physicality and dogfights are anathema; but I'm not so thrilled either with pee. Reminds me of . . . (Will she ever get out of this book?)

Thus I seem to have turned out to be—well—

not a dog whisperer or a dog murmurer or a dog wrangler or even much of a dog serenader. I seem to be more of a wussy kind of watchdog: watching with horror as my dogs are, well, dogs. Then, going belly up myself. I did love those terriers, though. I miss them every day. So please understand, small terrier gods, that it was horribly painful to part with Diva. Millard had been her slave. Norah and I had been her servants. But one thing about getting older: I know myself better. I know that I have to avoid the hard stuff. I need easy pets. Something like . . .

Turtles.

Ah, but I was so lucky to find our Deeviedog the absolutely perfect home; a home in the country with a wonderful young family who have a little boy and who let her chase birds and chipmunks in the woods and in general give her so much exercise that, now, instead of the waddle dog she was becoming with me, she could be the pinup dog on the weight-loss cover of some Special Pet Issue of *People*. Her adoring new owners tell me they've even bought her a carrier for car rides that "lifts her up high on the front seat so she can look out (and is less likely to throw up)." And she's doing a bit of obedience training, which is not, they say, "an overwhelming success." They also report that she still chases airplanes and barks at the highly threatening second hand on their kitchen clock. Not the brightest bulb in your Louis Seize chandelier, our Diva. But happy. Happy now.

I've been a little dim myself off and on, but here comes the happy ending.

Juno and Ajax and I are soldiering on.

We share a few beauty-filled rooms (you've guessed that) with scores of fine friends just nearby.

I date. And Juno and Ajax do, too, in the literal sense.

For instance, in her very old age (she's almost sixteen, our Juno; or 105+), she's begun to wee the moment she hits the sidewalk. Right in front of my upscale apartment building. It's washed away with water immediately, but of late, I've been harassed by a neighbor who "finds it unacceptable." "*My* dog is old," he says, "and she doesn't do things like that!" Drag her to the curb, he orders in his seven A.M. phone call (though, of course, that leaves a trail). Put a diaper on her in the elevator—she's obviously incontinent. (She's not.) Do something, he demands, because I'm not going to leave you alone. He's even sent someone from the building's board to visit me. The co-op police.

Communal living.

If I forget myself when the time comes, I hope no one drags me to the curb.

Ajax's face and back are white now, too, and he's had his city snags. As mild as my big sweet greyhound was, after a year in Manhattan he became terrified of every other dog on the sidewalk; not just his own sidewalk, but the one across the street, the one two blocks away and, basically, all the sidewalks clear up to the Bronx. In fact, who knows how far he sees? That's why they call them sight hounds.

Here's how this happened.

It took him a full year to feel comfortable with the rumble and screech of the buses in New York, the scream of the fire trucks, the thunder of the Harleys and those sireens' constant wail, not to mention the relentlessly approaching legs. Relatively comfortable, that is, because almost immediately, Ajax also became paranoid about everything on four legs with fur.

He knows each dog out there is out to get him. He slinks through the building's front door and looks both ways like it's seventies Gotham and he's waiting for a mugger. Fearfully, he checks behind him, on both sides and in doorways, and in his terror, he attacks. Labradors. Yorkies. Big dogs minding their own business. Little dogs minding other dogs' business. It's that old fight-or-flee response, but forget the flee: He's leashed. What's worse, because he can't bite a dog he can't reach, he strains to bite Juno or me. They call it referred aggression. But knowing its name doesn't help, and neither do pricey meds or reward training or anything at all but going out for walks at weird hours or retreating into the street where Ajax and Juno and I hide from other dogs behind parked cars and hope the cabs don't hit us. Ajax wears a muzzle on the street now, too, and I guess one of these days, when he edges around behind me and the Keystone Kops arrive, I'll sort my photos and write a memoir.

And wait for Seven Fat Years.

Meanwhile, I kiss my dogs every day and don't get fleas. I dole out their meds and treats. I see lots and lots of movies. And my life is good and dull.

Still, I dream myself a film from time to time. I dream of my lovely dogs. Of someone showing up at the door with a sweet-tempered Jack. Of lovely roses and needy houses. I dream of white summer porches and dazzling sunsets and cool mown grass and arching mulberries and rippling, sparkling harbors. Of dimpled southerners.

I dream of a mythic Paradise where good dogs—and good men—have golden tales.

Acknowledgments

For her careful reading; Paula Brancato

For her warm and touchingly diplomatic reading; fellow dog-lover Barbara King

For her politic, empathetic (and speedy!) reading; Dylan Landis

For her incisive reading and promise not to die first; Carolan Workman

For her tough, pet-centric reading; Emma Sweeney

For her enthusiasm, support, and encouragement from the get-go; Megan Newman

And finally,

For her concept; apologies, and profound gratitude to Elizabeth von Arnim